Running the Race

looking to Jesus for ultimate victory

Judson Edwards

BROADMAN PRESS
Nashville, Tennessee

Dewey Decimal Classification: 248.4
Subject Headings: CHRISTIAN LIFE
Library of Congress Catalog Number: 85-4700

Printed in the United States of America

Unless otherwise stated, all Scripture quotations are from the Revised Standard Version of the Bible, copyrighted 1946, 1952, © 1971, 1973.

Scripture quotations marked KJV are from the King James Version of the Bible.

Library of Congress Cataloging in Publication Data

Edwards, Judson.
  Running the race.

  Bibliography: p.
  1. Christian life—Baptist authors.   2. Running in the Bible.   I. Title.
BV4501.2.E316   1985   248.4′86132   85-4700
ISBN 0-8054-5711-9 (pbk.)

To my parents,
Travis and Irene Edwards,
who gave me a running start in the race.

Contents

On Your Mark . . .
    Introduction 11
Get Set . . .
  1. Knowing the Race 17
  2. Anticipating the Hurdles 27
  3. Running to Win 42
Go . . .
  4. The Start 57
  5. Running in the Pack 70
  6. Crowd Noise 82
  7. Falling Back 95
  8. Second Wind 107
  9. Picking Up the Pace 119
10. Gun Lap 133
11. The Winner's Stand 145

On Your Mark, . . .

The gun is up! The runners walk to the starting line, breathing deeply to relieve the tension. The race will soon begin.

Introduction

I saw her again this morning when I went out to get the newspaper. Dressed in a baggy, gray sweat suit, she was making her usual morning run. Every time I see her, I marvel at her discipline. She obviously will never be a competitive marathoner. Her stride is uneven, and her running style resembles that of a camel. But that doesn't seem to dull her commitment to running. Up and down the street she lopes, day after day. She is a part of "the running generation."

Others jog by my house, too. Men and women of all shapes, sizes, and ages stride by our place on the corner. Most of them are victims of the running boom that hit our country several years ago. They have paid high prices for special shoes, read the "in" books on running, and established a schedule of personal goals. They jog daily around tracks and neighborhoods, looking primarily for health and peace of mind.

I, too, became a runner a couple of years ago. I started inconspicuously in Bermuda shorts and boat shoes but now have upgraded my gear. I now have several pair of in-style running shorts, a pair of good, cushioned shoes, two running suits for cold weather, and a watch with a stopwatch function. Every day but Sunday, I can be seen dashing (plodding?) through the neighborhood, putting in my miles. Some onlookers admire my quest for fitness. Others, I'm sure, question my sanity.

I've even entered quite a few "fun runs" and have a drawerful of colorful T-shirts given to participants in those races. I'm still seeking my first trophy for winning one, however. To be painfully honest, I have much more in common with my camel-loping neighbor than I do with Alberto Salazar or Bill Rodgers. But I am a full-fledged runner, nonetheless.

In 1977 the late James Fixx wrote a book entitled *The Complete Book of Running*. The book became a publishing phenomenon and was followed by a sequel, appropriately called *Jim Fixx's Second Book of Running*. Both books are addressed to those of us who run and want to know more about our sport, and both books provide needed motivation and information.

I thought about calling this book *The Complete Book of Running the Christian Race* but decided that might be too "cute." Besides, I'm not sure any book other than the Bible should carry such a designation! I do want us to look at the "running" passages in the Bible in these pages, because they provide such a fascinating way of looking at the Christian pilgrimage. I hope to use these Scriptures to impart some motivation and some information as we seek to live for Jesus Christ.

When the idea for this book first tapped me on the shoulder, I ran from it (no pun intended!). I did not want to write a frothy "jogging for Jesus" manual and link Christianity with the current running craze. Better not to write at all, I reasoned, than to write trivia.

But the more I considered a book based on the "running" passages, the more substance it seemed to have. I came to see these verses as a unique means of looking at the Christian life from start to finish. My hope is that you will be helped by this unusual vantage point.

Certainly, the biblical writers were not afraid to use running as a metaphor of the spiritual life. The psalmist, the prophets Isaiah and Jeremiah, the Preacher in Ecclesiastes, the apostle Paul, and the writer of the Book of Hebrews all used the imagery of running a race to describe the journey with God. These men probably had witnessed Olympic-like festivals where running was featured and saw something in the struggle to win a race that reminded them of their own spiritual journeys.

If you are a runner—and some sources indicate there are nearly thirty million in America—I think you will find the "running" metaphors of Scripture intriguing. If you are not a runner, I hope you will not discard this book as irrelevant. Remember, it is about living for Christ in the modern world, and even if you despise running, I trust there is something here that can instruct or inspire you.

I'd like to think the book will help all of us—runners and nonrunners alike—to run better "the race that is set before us" (Heb. 12:1).

Get Set, . . .

The runners wait in taut anticipation for the gun to sound. The impending race consumes their thoughts. They know their success will depend on three factors: a knowledge of the race, an anticipation of the hurdles, and a confident attitude. They concentrate on these three factors as they wait for the starter's gun.

1.
Knowing the Race

*"If you have raced with men on foot,
and they have wearied you,
how will you compete with horses?"* (Jer. 12:5).

Imagine the folly of a runner on the starting line with no inkling as to the nature of the race. Poised, waiting for the gun to crack, he has no idea whether his race is a hundred-yard dash or a three-mile run. The prospects for success for such a runner are slim indeed! Because he doesn't know his race, he can have no strategy for running it well. He will fail because of ignorance.

Jesus was explicit in His directions for beginning the Christian race. Count the cost, He taught, lest you be like the man who started construction of a tower and ran out of money before its completion. Count the cost, He said, lest you be like the king who went to battle with a dangerous shortage of soldiers. In other words, know something about the race before you step to the starting line!

Misconceptions about the Christian race abound. One of the more popular ones is the idea that Christianity offers an easy escape from the woes and worries of life. The image of Christianity depicted on many a page and screen is that of carefree, Spirit-filled ecstasy. Christians are presented as bubbly people who sail above the traumas of ordinary living. They are, it would seem, immune to tragedy, doubt, boredom, and depression. And they greet every day with a sweet grin and a resounding "Praise the Lord!"

As inviting as that notion is, it just will not square with either biblical revelation or personal experience. In the Bible—fine, committed people get knocked around by life in spite of, or because of, their faith; and in life—good, Christian folks experience disaster, hurt, and unthinkable evil. Christianity as an aspirin tablet that eases all pain simply will not fit the facts.

The prophet Jeremiah learned this from his own experiences and honestly shared his discoveries in the biblical book that bears his name. The prophet of old can help us moderns gain insight into the nature of the race before us.

The particular verse under consideration is a reply to the prophet from God. "[Jeremiah]" God inquires, "if you have raced with men on foot, and they have wearied you, how will you compete with horses?"

That pointed and surprising question follows a query Jeremiah had posed to God about the nature of life. The prophet's question is reminiscent of the questions Job asked God and was asked with urgency and utmost sincerity. There was nothing nonchalant about the question the prophet raised: "Why does the way of the wicked prosper?" (Jer. 12:1).

Underneath that question there was a lot of emotion. Jeremiah did not want to debate philosophy; he wanted to know why life had been so unfair to him *personally.* In the previous chapter, the prophet had indicated that a few of his fellow Jews had plotted to take his life (see 11:8-10). For all of his commitment and bold proclamation, what was his reward? An attempt on his life! And for all of his faithful devotion to God, what did he receive? Imprisonment, ridicule, and harassment!

No, underneath that query as to why the wicked prosper, there was a deep personal hurt. Jeremiah was really asking, "Why does a godly man know such pain, while evil men know such prosperity? Why is this happening to me, of all people? And why don't you do something, God, to balance the scales and establish justice?"

Those were difficult, serious questions from an obedient but perplexed man of faith. As hard and demanding as those questions were, though, they were at least honest. Jeremiah's questions, for all their skepticism, were better than the sweet, smiling faith that is afraid to look reality in the eye. It is better to be an honest searcher than a dishonest know-it-all.

Well, it would seem that God would surely step forth and vindicate Himself to the hurting, seeking prophet. Surely this was the time for a divine treatise on evil and suffering in the world and why justice seems to be on such frequent vacations. Surely God would now tell Jeremiah the secret to the mystery of life's hurts.

But He didn't. In fact, the answer the prophet heard running around in his head was not an answer at all. Like Job, Jeremiah didn't receive an explanation—it was a challenge.

He heard God ask in rebuttal, "If you have raced with men on foot and been exhausted, how can you compete with horses?" In essence, "Jeremiah, if this has gotten you down, what will you do when the going really gets tough? If you are discouraged and grumbling about this little race with footmen, how in the world will you respond when you have to run with speedy horses?" Looking for explanation or consolation, the perplexed prophet got exhortation! "Get up and keep running!" he heard God thunder.

Now we can only guess what Jeremiah learned about faith's race from God's surprising question. Obviously he learned that his faith in God did not exempt him from pain and struggle. But I can think of three other truths

Jeremiah probably learned—three truths we, too, can learn as we ponder the race before us.

A Race to Be Run

First, the race is to be run, not understood. It's ironic, isn't it? One of the truths we must know about the Christian life is: We can't know everything about it! Paradoxically, we must learn that we will never learn it all. Mired in self-pity and wanting logical answers, Jeremiah must have learned this fundamental truth: A journey with God is a journey of trust, even when you don't understand life's puzzlements. Sometimes you just have to run, even though you don't comprehend all of the twists and turns in the track.

A passage from Isaiah stresses this same concept and reminds us that we will never comprehend all of God's ways:

> For my thoughts are not your thoughts,
> neither are your ways my ways, says the Lord.
> For as the heavens are higher than the earth,
> so are my ways higher than your ways
> and my thoughts than your thoughts (Isa. 55:8-9).

God's ways are different from ours, and His thoughts are lifted up high above even the keenest of human minds. So we follow Him, even though we don't always understand Him. We gamely run with footmen and horses, even though, like Jeremiah, we sometimes find ourselves doubting and grumbling about our experiences.

With all due respect to Christian apologists and biblical expositors, we must understand that much about the Christian life cannot be explained. Mystery often reigns supreme. Try as we may to comprehend prayer, the Trinity, the atonement, Christ's second coming, our own experiences, and other doctrines, we always come up short. The Bible refuses to be a computer printout, and God shuns all of our microscopes.

Certainly we must study the Bible to know its life-changing truths; certainly we must come to personal convictions about doctrine and theology; certainly we must preach, teach, and live God's Word before humanity. But we must also be aware that much of our experience with God is beyond our capacity to understand and explain. Like Paul, we now see "through a glass darkly" ["a mirror dimly"] now, and we live with the knowledge that our faith is to be lived, not dissected.

Until we realize that faith is for living, we will sit in indecision trying to figure out everything about God and never get into the race. It is crucial for us to know that we cannot know it all! We can believe by faith that God loves us, that Christ died for us, and that we must open our lives to God's offer of salvation; but to think we must have knowledge of the intricate details of God's mind is a sure indication that we'll never enter the race.

One preacher commented that we can put off making up our minds, but that we can't put off making up our lives. He's right. We must live today. Our commitment to Christ is for today. Whether or not we have all of the theological answers is not the real test of our faith. Rather, that test is whether or not it sees us victoriously through the experiences of this day.

When he wanted to debate, argue, and complain, Jeremiah was cut off by God's abrupt reply. "The race is for running, Jeremiah. Life is for living. Sometimes you have to maintain the pace, even when the footmen and horses seem to be certain winners."

A Distance Race

There is a second idea I think we can learn from God's question to Jeremiah. A journey with God is a distance race and not a sprint. I like the title of one of Eugene Peterson's books: *A Long Obedience in the Same Direction.* That is an apt description of the Christian race. As Jesus put it, anyone who follows Him had better be ready to put his hand to the plow and keep it there. Christianity is not for fickle followers. Discipleship is not for the easily discouraged.

Jeremiah's plea for explanation of his plight fell on deaf ears. The answer God gave only promised further, more demanding trials down the pike. Rather than feeling a reassuring pat on the back and a consoling promise that his struggle would soon be over, Jeremiah was beckoned by God to consider the long haul. God called him to look beyond the pesky footmen to see the fleet horses that wanted to vie with him in the future. God's question focused Jeremiah's eyes on the distant horizon and assured him of more races later on.

After that disturbing question, the man of God knew he had better be ready for "a long obedience."

Church rolls are typically crowded with people who "dropped out" because they didn't understand that the Christian race is a long-distance run. Most of them began with a burst of emotional energy. They sprinted down an aisle and then rushed into church attendance, Sunday school classes, and committee assignments. But then the other church members didn't befriend them properly. The preacher's theology was misguided. The music was too "high church." Or the softball team started to quarrel. So, they grew discouraged, discarded their church duties over trivia, and eventually drifted off into uselessness.

What's the problem here? Why this defection from the Christian community? Why this turning away from Christ? It can be traced to a basic misunderstanding of the spiritual life. These dropouts failed to consider their commitment to Christ and His church as "a long obedience in the same direction." Sure, some church people are snobbish; some preachers' theology is atrocious; some music is stuffy; and most softball teams bicker. But if those little things drive us from the service of Christ, our understanding of Christian commitment is shallow indeed! If these sluggish footmen mess us up, what will we do when life's horses (disease, depression, divorce, and the like) suddenly confront us?

Last year, I entered a ten-kilometer (6.2 miles) race near my home. Several hundred of us gathered early one March morning at the local city hall, claimed our race packets, pinned our numbers on our shirts, and did an assortment of stretching exercises. As the 8 AM starting time approached, we huddled at the starting line and received our final instructions. Then the gun sounded, and we started slowly down the road.

All but one of us, that is. One young man—in his early twenties, I would guess, and built like a tailback—sprinted quickly into the lead. His time for the first quarter mile must have been under sixty seconds! The rest of us watched his sprint in disbelief. Either he had never run a 10-K before, or we were preparing to see a new world's record! Shortly, he disappeared from sight.

I saw him again at the 5-K mark, and he scarcely looked like the same runner! Arms flailing and chest heaving, he was moving at a turtle's pace. As I passed him, I heard him panting like a locomotive and wheezing like a teapot. He did finish the race but far back in the pack!

That runner, sadly, has a spiritual counterpart. Many

people have started the Christian pilgrimage with a flash of brilliance. They look, to all the world, like spiritual record setters. But they fail to account for the long haul. They seem to think that the start of the race is not as important as the finish. So, they struggle to life's end exhausted and useless. They were good sprinters, but the race was a long run, and they were not ready for it.

To all who would entertain the notion of running the Christian race, Christ's words give pointed, needed counsel: "He who endures to the end will be saved" (Matt. 10:22).

A Lap at a Time

There is a third truth concealed in God's question to Jeremiah: the idea that the race will be won a lap at a time. Let me ask you an important question: How do we prepare ourselves to run with horses? To put it more plainly, how do we equip ourselves to handle the crises and heavy pressures that are sure to come?

The answer is in God's question to the prophet. We learn to run with horses by first running with footmen! We prepare to handle the big crises of life by learning to handle the little ones. Someone has rightly observed that we can't beg a fiddle today and play a concert in Carnegie Hall tomorrow. We can't expect to conquer the real tragedies of life unless we respond well to the minor irritations that dog us daily.

Now, it is obvious from the number of irritations most of us have to face that we have ample opportunity for training! Those pesky footmen are everywhere! Daily they stalk us, trying to lure us into anger or depression.

In his book *Creative Brooding*, Robert Raines told of a priest who regularly heard the confessions of a group of nuns. After hearing their confessions all day, the priest declared it was like being stoned to death with popcorn!

Most of us know the feeling. The kids are loud, the job is demanding, the arthritis flares up occasionally, the traffic is irksome, etc., etc., etc. We feel like we're being stoned to death with popcorn.

But in responding well to those molehills we learn to scale the mountains. The Christian race is a daily affair. It is usually not dramatic or spectacular. We work; we play; we love our families; we minister when we can; we serve our church; we pray for change and growth. In short, we do a bunch of ordinary, human activities, but how well we do them and how much love we put into them determines our character. We are shaped, you see, by the ordinary.

So it is important for us to run patiently with the footmen, to run the race a lap at a time. How one runs today determines the kind of runner one will be tomorrow. We cannot be idle and shiftless day after day and expect to run like champions when the pressure hits. The race is such that it must be run a lap at a time, and if we don't handle the minor trifles, we'll never manage the major tragedies.

There came a time in Jesus' life when He had to run with horses. In the garden of Gethsemane, He agonized over the cross. Because He was fully man, yet also fully God, He didn't want to die such a death. The cross would be excruciatingly painful, but infinitely worse would be bearing the ignominy of mankind's sins. But He didn't run from the cross, and He didn't lash out at His accusers. In the face of pressure, evil, and death itself, He responded with a courageous composure that still astounds us when we read about it. He died not cursing His executioners, but forgiving them.

Why? Why did He endure that agony with such grace? Because He had learned daily how to handle pressure! In the wilderness, Satan had tantalized Him with alluring temptations, but Jesus didn't give in to that pressure. He refused to nibble on evil's offer. Throughout His ministry, Jesus had dined on a steady diet of conflict, tension, and misunderstanding. But He always responded with love, sometimes escaping to the countryside for rest, sometimes telling delightful stories to explain His truths, and sometimes confronting lazy thinking with blunt assertions. Jesus faced the cross with grace because He had responded to life's everyday tensions with grace. By running well with footmen, He was well-equipped to race with horses.

As we think about our own irritability, frustration, depression, and discouragement, God's question to Jeremiah gives us pause: If we have run with footmen and been wearied, how can we expect to compete with horses?

The Christian life must be lived with love and courage each day. Every day we live is another lap around the track. And how well we run each lap ultimately determines our success in the race as a whole.

God's surprising question to Jeremiah is a good place to begin our probing of the Christian race. It tells us what to expect along the way. Like the prophet of old, we cannot expect to be exempted from the hurts and pressures of life. Even though we may be people of faith, we will have to contend with footmen, and sometimes we will have to run with horses.

But because we are prepared for the race, we can meet the challenge. We can run with faith, even when we don't comprehend the journey. We can run with endurance because we are aware that the race is a long one. And we can run each lap diligently, knowing that the race will be won one lap at a time.

2.
Anticipating the Hurdles

". . . lest somehow I should be running or had run in vain"
(*Gal. 2:2*).
*". . . so that in the day of Christ I may be proud that I did
not run in vain or labor in vain"* (*Phil. 2:16*).

There is an ominous possibility raised in these two statements from Paul's pen. "Running in vain" suggests the
possibility of a futile race. The phrase conjures up the
image of a valiant runner who somehow is thrown off
course and never completes the journey. For whatever
reason, the runner becomes sidetracked and ends up
"running in vain."

What would cause that? Why would a well-intentioned
Christian pilgrim veer off course? What would make a
sincere Christian stumble into uselessness and dejection?

Hurdles! There are hurdles all along the Christian Way
that can trip us up and send us sprawling. In Chapter 1,
we saw that the Christian race is a long-distance run. In
this chapter, I want us to realize that there are hurdles
lurking on the track, too. To prepare well for the race, we
must anticipate these hurdles lest they catch us by surprise. For if we are ignorant of the hurdles, we all too
easily can wind up "running in vain."

In John Bunyan's classic allegory, *The Pilgrim's
Progress,* "Pilgrim" is confronted with obstacle after obstacle on his journey to "The Celestial City." The pathway
is lined with problems and temptations. Pilgrim's path is
dangerous, for he has constantly to surmount these obstacles.

Bunyan's allegory tells us that the Way is hazardous! Obstacles and hurdles line the track! All of us who run the Christian race need to be aware of these barriers, or frustration and defeat will be our constant companions.

What are the hurdles we must clear? First of all, they will vary from person to person. Flip through the whole catalog of sins and temptations, and you will discover all of the hurdles that can cause us to "run in vain."

Lust, greed, pride, and selfishness are among the biggest hurdles we have to jump. Doubt looms large in many lives. Depression trips up many a game runner. A rigid, legalistic attitude sends a number of pilgrims sprawling. Even such a seemingly innocent problem as shyness prevents many of us from reaching our potential for Christ. To put it tersely, there is no shortage of hurdles!

But from the bulging catalog of sins and temptations, I want to pull out four of the more subtle obstacles and examine them. These hurdles, though subtle, are devastating. Any one of them can ruin our effectiveness for Christ. The four hurdles I want us to notice are conformity, insensitivity, overfamiliarity, and clutter.

The Hurdle of Conformity

Conformity is the scourge of the Christian life. "Be not conformed," Paul exhorted the early Roman church (see Rom. 12:1-2). The person who pledges allegiance to Jesus Christ really aligns himself with what I call "biblical nonconformity." Everything is different in the Christian realm! Values, attitudes, priorities, finances, activities, and relationships all assume a different hue in the Christian's life.

In my first book, *A Matter of Choice*, (1983, Broadman) I sketched nine areas in which Christians are different from the world around them. That book merely scratched the surface. The follower of Christ lives a distinctive life! Every facet of his life bears the stamp of nonconformity.

If we truly want to understand the kind of sweeping changes Christ wants for our lives, the best place to look is the Sermon on the Mount. In the sermon, Jesus spells out quite plainly what it means to be a citizen of God's kingdom. In bold and flashing strokes, He paints a picture of a society drastically different from the one in which we now live. Even for Christians, His words are shocking and revolutionary because they stand in sharp contrast to who we are and how we live. Gerald Mann indicted us when he wrote:

> The Sermon on the Mount makes us nervous because its teachings are X-rated—in the sense that the Christian world has never dared to take them seriously. Christians have constantly pawned them off as dated, impractical, and idealistic. Instead of using them to change culture, we have allowed culture to change them. And the result is that we have yet to catch up with the world-transforming power which Jesus proclaimed.[1]

If we are ever going to obtain that world-transforming power, and if we are ever going to be different from the world, we will have to understand and heed what Jesus teaches in Matthew 5—7. His words sketch the outline of a new order. They prescribe a totally new way of approaching life. And they remind us, every time we read them, what it means to be Christian.

The Sermon on the Mount comes best into focus, I think, when it is seen as a picture of conversion. Jesus delineates what it means to be converted to His new Way by telling us what to "turn from" and what to "turn to." In repentance we *turn from* some things, and in faith we *turn to* some others. These individual "turnings" show how a Christian is different from the world.

Fifteen such "turnings" are evident in the Sermon on the Mount. Paul stated in 2 Corinthians 5:17 that "if any one is in Christ, he is a new creation; the old has passed away, behold, the new has come." In Matthew 5—7, Jesus gives us the specifics of the "new" that has come. Those who know Him are to turn from the old world to the new one He came to establish.

By glancing briefly at these fifteen "turnings," we can better understand how to clear the hurdle of conformity. Followers of Jesus are to turn from:

(1) The popular concept of happiness to a radically different one (5:3-12).—Eight qualities of a "blessed" or happy person are listed in the Beatitudes. They are so foreign to contemporary concepts of happiness, we can scarcely comprehend them.

(2) Indifference to influence (5:13-16).—The "new Way" is inhabited by men and women who are "salt" and "light" and who, by their deeds of love, reflect God to the world.

(3) Lawlessness to righteousness (5:17-20).—Those who are a part of this new Kingdom know, practice, and teach God's commandments.

(4) Anger to reconciliation (5:21-26).—Attitude as well as action is important in the new world Christ founded. Not only murder, but even an attitude of divisive anger, is forbidden. The goal is harmony and reconciliation.

(5) Lust to faithful love (5:27-32).—Adultery has always been forbidden, but the new order also forbids lust. There is no place in Christ's kingdom for looking at others through eyes of manipulative self-gratification.

(6) Double-talk to simple truth (5:33-37).—No lies, dou-

ble-talk, or half-truths are allowed. In the "new world," speak simply and with integrity.

(7) Revenge to grace (5:38-42).—The ethic of the "old world" was and is "an eye for an eye and a tooth for a tooth." The "new Way" is of grace—turning the other cheek, offering the cloak to an angry comrade, walking the extra mile, and giving gladly to the obnoxious beggar.

(8) Hatred to love of enemies (5:43-48).—It is only natural to love your friends and hate your enemies. But this new Kingdom is built around *agape*, a sacrificing, God-like love that embraces everyone. It is the nature of *agape* to break down dividing walls so that enemies become friends.

(9) Showiness to secret devotion (6:1-18).—"Worldly" religion flaunts its devotion. It gives money to the poor when others can see and appreciate it, prays eloquently when others are listening, and fasts when others can applaud its sacrifice. Jesus recommends secret, private devotion before an audience of One.

(10) Accumulation of possessions to abandonment to God (6:19-24).—In the battle for our affection, Jesus advocates God over money. The "old world" has always judged a person's success by the size of his bank account. The "new world" judges it by their love for the Lord.

(11) Anxiety to trust (6:25-34).—The birds of the air and the lilies of the field are symbols of life in Christ's kingdom. They do not worry; they trust. And that kind of trustful peace is the legacy of all who live in Christ's world.

(12) Judging others to honest self-scrutiny (7:1-6).—Suspicion, criticism, and blame are trademarks of the world. The follower of Christ has no time for such activities. He can't worry about the speck in another's eye. He has all he can handle in picking the log from his own eye.

(13) Uncertainty to confident prayer (7:7-12).—Overseeing life in the new order is a loving Father who wants to give freely to all who ask. Therefore, citizens of this Kingdom can come confidently to Him and be blessed.

(14) Talk to action (7:13-23).—Citizens of the world talk, plan, form committees, rationalize, and procrastinate. Citizens of the Kingdom don't talk much; they *act*, simply and promptly.

(15) The "sand" of society to the "rock" of a new Way (7:24-29)—Jesus concludes His charter for a new society with the parable of the house on the sand and the house on the rock. Though His Way seems strange and unlikely, and though His Kingdom is not heavily populated, He asserts that His Way is indestructible. Those who build their lives on the truths He has outlined are building on a sturdy rock that cannot be destroyed.

These "turnings" provide the marching orders we need to move on with the business of building a new society. And they spell out how the Christian is to "be not conformed to this world." Unfortunately, this Way seems strange and even naïve to us as Christians because we have become so accustomed to life as our world lives it. Jesus' words shake us and disturb us because we realize how many "turnings" we still need to make.

Jim Wallis reminds us that ours is really an "upside down" Kingdom:

> To put it mildly, the Sermon on the Mount offers a way of life contrary to what we are accustomed. It overturns our assumptions of what is normal, reasonable, and responsible. To put it more bluntly, the Sermon stands our values on their heads.[2]

The gospel has always stood society's values on their

heads. So, the follower of Jesus Christ is not to be conformed to the outside world.

But let's go even further in our understanding of biblical nonconformity. The Christian is also not to be conformed to other Christians! Even though we might share a common Lord, a common Bible, and a common church with another person, we will not share a common pilgrimage. God has a unique adventure for every runner!

No one else will ever have exactly your relationship with the Father. Your experiences, struggles, thoughts, and personal relationships will be uniquely your own. God never uses a copier to make saints, and He never gives birth to spiritual twins. Each of us has a special race to run.

When we try to squeeze into someone else's mold, we deny the special work God wants to do in and through us. In Christ, we are free—free to search for truth, free to develop our own theology, free to find our own style of worship, free to be who we are.

Tragically, the pressure to conform to a certain stereotype strangles the individuality out of many Christians. Lively, fun-loving people become somber religionists because of peer pressure. Inquisitive, creative people become religious parrots mimicking church leaders because of the pressure to conform. We can be eternally grateful that Jesus, Paul, Peter, and the other early church leaders were free enough to shed the handcuffs of conformity!

Christ Jesus has set us free! We are free to be different from the world and free to be different from our fellow believers. The only yoke upon us is the one we gladly accepted when we made Jesus our Lord.

The Hurdle of Insensitivity

Jesus was known for His sensitivity. Even in a milling crowd of people, He was sensitive enough to feel the touch of a hurting woman in need of healing. Even though the religious leaders of His day were ready to stone an adulteress, Jesus was sensitive enough to see her deep need of forgiveness. Even though the streets of Jericho were crowded with noisy people, Jesus was sensitive enough to single out one lonely man named Zacchaeus perched on the limb of a sycamore tree. Even though the soldiers who nailed Him to the cross were hardened and cruel, Jesus was sensitive enough to see their desperate need for forgiving love.

The Gospels are unanimous in showing us this: Jesus was a perceptive, caring Person. And He told His followers, "As the Father has sent me, even so I send you" (John 20:21).

His followers are to be known by their love, the same kind of sensitive love He displayed. But Christian love—that reads between the lines, that sees the hurts and hopes in people's eyes, that reaches out—must be developed. It does not come automatically with church membership or faithful worship attendance. It is possible to memorize the whole Bible and not be sensitive to people. It is possible to expound God's Word every week from pulpit or lectern and yet be numb to the pain of the people being addressed. Seminaries can teach theology, music, and education easier than they can teach sensitivity. Neither can churches teach it easily, though they can nurture it. Ultimately, developing Jesus' kind of sensitivity is a lengthy, individual project.

How do we develop it? My answer to that question sounds so elementary I am almost embarrassed to put it into writing. We can increase our sensitivity if we will follow the advice we learned as nursery children: stop, look, and listen. Before we write off those three words as a slogan only for preschoolers learning to cross the street, let us consider how stopping, looking, and listening apply to us as adults in need of sensitivity.

Stop. We can stop focusing all of our attention on ourselves. We can stop thinking that "real living" is acquiring a load of personal "goodies." We can stop running around in a frenzy, trying to "accomplish something." We can stop doing all of the trivial things that waste our days. We can stop relating to people the way everyone else does. We can stop being afraid of people and start trying to trust them.

Look. We can look at the people in our lives—at church, at ball practice, at home. We can look at their hands and eyes and learn much about who they really are. We can look at the way they walk and the clothes they wear. We can look beneath the surface for hidden feelings.

Listen. We can listen to our child's account of his day at school and our neighbor's hopes for her children. We can listen to the joy of the woman who has just had a baby and the agony of the man who has learned he has cancer. We can listen to the concerto of human sounds all around us, and we will be amazed at what we will learn about people.

If all of this seems too simple, and we are charged by sophisticates with being naïve, our best response is that we are only following Jesus. Our methodology comes from the One who *stopped* that day under the sycamore tree, *looked* up and saw Zacchaeus, and *listened* to him long enough to change his life.

Somewhere along the way the hurdle of insensitivity will confront us. Much in our day lulls us into this numbness to others. The frenzied pace of our lives prevents us from drinking coffee with neighbors and fishing with friends. The "looking-out-for-number-one" philosophy discourages closeness at the office. Job pressures, church meetings, housework, homework, Little League, video games, ad infinitum—keep us from intimacy at home. It is not easy to stop, look, and listen in today's society. We will have to struggle against the status quo to develop sensitivity.

But if we are to follow Jesus, we must. If we are to mature as His disciples, we will have to do more than attend church and memorize Bible verses. We will have to be attentive to people and try to touch them with compassion the way He always did, and does.

The Hurdle of Overfamiliarity

It may be going too far to mention that, in the Christian life, familiarity breeds contempt. It is not going too far, however, to admit that familiarity does breed *indifference*. A third hurdle in the Christian race is the hurdle of overfamiliarity. And if that hurdle is not cleared, the runner falls headlong into boredom.

There eventually develops a "here-we-go-again" mentality in the Christian faith. After all, we reach the point where we've heard nearly all of the biblical stories and memorized most of the songs in the hymnal. The preacher passionately tells us about the prodigal son lost in a far country, but we already know the ending to that one, and it doesn't move us anymore. We read "God is love" from the First Epistle of John, but we've heard that so much it's "old hat." The evangelist urges us to repent, but isn't that what they all say? Because we are familiar with the ways of the church and the message of the Bible, we are lulled into indifference. We know the right answers, and our theology is definitely orthodox, but there is no life in us!

This is no new problem. Soren Kierkegaard, writing to nineteenth-century Christians in Denmark, saw that their problem was the dullness caused by overfamiliarity:

> Everyone with some capacity of observation, who serious-ly considers what is called Christendom, or the conditions in a so-called Christian country, must surely be assailed by profound misgivings. What does it mean that all these thousands call themselves Christians as a matter of course?[3]

Kierkegaard saw many names on the church rolls but little fire in the pews!

To speak to his lifeless comrades, he once related a story of a group of geese in a barnyard. Every seventh day these geese marched to a corner of the yard. Then their most persuasive orator jumped on the fence and spoke elo-quently concerning the wonders of geese. He chronicled the valiant exploits of their forefathers who had flown high in the sky. He praised God for making geese and giving them wings to fly. All of the geese in the yard listened intently and nodded solemnly. One thing they did not do, however. They never flew themselves, for the corn was good and the barnyard cozy.

When overfamiliarity trips us up, all we can do is stum-ble to the corner of the yard and talk of yesteryear. The thought of taking up wings and actually flying never crosses our minds.

I have an old lawnmower that occasionally decides not to run. I have tinkered with it, though, and know the problem now. After continued use, black crust gathers on the spark plug. It builds up a little bit at a time until finally the plug is so congested it gets no spark. When my mower refuses to start, I know it is time to clean the spark plug and wipe away the crusty deposits that have built up over a period of time.

That, in effect, is what happens to us spiritually. We run here and there doing our "spiritual" things—reading the Bible, praying, attending church, teaching Sunday School, going to concerts by Christian singers, but somehow the black crust of familiarity begins to choke out our vitality. The freshness of faith leaves us and, in its place, we find a stale routine. Our problem is not that the good news is no longer "good" to us. Our problem is that it's no longer "news" to us! We're not surprised by God anymore!

When this deadening routine sets in, it is time to wipe away the layers of built-up orthodoxy and celebrate again the simplicity of our gospel. Celebrate it: The God of the universe takes delight in you! He wants you to experience joy. He wants you to love people. He wants you to forget your works so you can be surprised again by the wonder of grace. He wants you to clean your life of all your accumulated filth—sin, worry, struggle for status, and desire to be impressive—to experience Him.

Only when we periodically return to the simplicity of the gospel can we remove the awful burden of trying to be "religious." We are loved! All of our service to God is in response to His loving us first (see 1 John 4:19). Acknowledging that we can never give enough, know enough, witness enough, pray enough, or be good enough is the first step toward recovering the spiritual spark.

The Hurdle of Clutter

Simplicity is a rare quality these days. A complex, tangled world is producing complex, tangled individuals. (Or is it the other way around?) When you do meet someone who lives simply, you notice an attractive freedom about that person. Simplicity is actually an insignia of liberty.

A fourth hurdle most Christians discover on the track is clutter. We are tempted to immerse ourselves in the many mad pursuits of the world. Quite unintentionally, we discover our lives cluttered with trivia. We do all of the "in" things, buy all of the "in" contraptions, and go to all of the "in" places. But meaning eludes us, and faith slowly disintegrates.

In one of His parables, Jesus clearly warns us against the peril of clutter. In the parable, a sower plants seed. Some falls on hard ground and never takes root. Some falls into shallow soil with no nutrients and quickly withers. But it is the third kind of soil in Jesus' parable I want to underscore here: the cluttered soil. "Other seed fell among thorns and the thorns grew up and choked it, and it yielded no grain" (Mark 4:7). And just what do these thorns represent?

> And others are the ones sown among the thorns; they are those who hear the word, but the cares of the world, and the delight in riches, and the desire for other things, enter in and choke the word, and it proves unfruitful (Mark 4:18-19).

Jesus is teaching that the cluttered heart eventually chokes out the Word of God. The Word takes root and sprouts, but cares, riches, and desires smother it. God's intention for that person is strangled by trivia. God's Word for that man or woman is replaced by the graffiti of the world. Conversion is stifled by clutter.

The Jesus Way is the simple Way. Most of what He taught is shocking in its simplicity. Seek first God's kingdom. Deny self. Love others. Give freely. Pray confidently. Trust God. Those are simple statements prescribing a simple life-style. And He validated His words by living simply and freely Himself.

We now believe that more is always better. The more food, activities, relationships, and money—the better, we think. But it is time for us to realize that more is not always better. Do we always need more in our lives? Or is it possible that following Jesus would prompt us to think small, to shed some nonessentials for the sake of simplicity? Could we do and be better with fewer entanglements and fewer possessions? Would the race be smoother if we traveled lighter?

When I was an aspiring track star in high school, I frequently trained with weights strapped to my ankles. Those weights made for some difficult running! But when I removed them, it felt as if I could fly down the track. My not-too-speedy times verify that I actually didn't do much flying. I simply felt free and unencumbered without those nagging weights.

If only we could shed the self-imposed weights we now carry, we would be shocked at how easy and enjoyable life can be. Free from the load of too much food, too many activities, too many material goods, and too much unnecessary pressure, we would be able to "seek first the kingdom of God." We would have time for relationships, money for ministry, and energy for witnessing.

We would begin celebrating the liberty simplicity would bring us. And we might even find ourselves singing an old Shaker song because it expresses our own joyous discovery:

> 'Tis a gift to be simple,
> 'Tis a gift to be free,
> 'Tis a gift to come down
> where we ought to be,

And when you find yourself in the place just right,
'Twill be in a valley of love and delight!

When true simplicity is gained,
To live and to love we shan't be ashamed,
To turn, turn will be our delight,
Till by turning, turning,
We turn 'round right.[4]

Conformity, insensitivity, overfamiliarity, and clutter
are four of the hurdles we will have to jump in the race
before us. Other hurdles will also be present, but these
four seem to me especially common and subtle.

Hopefully, by anticipating them in advance, we will be
able to clear them and keep on moving. They will un-
doubtedly reappear further down the track, and we will
have to jump them again and again. But jump them we
will because, like Paul, we shudder to think of hitting a
hurdle, taking a spill, and "running in vain."

3.

Running to Win

"Do you not know that in a race all the runners compete, but only one receives the prize? So run that you may obtain it" (1 Cor. 9:24).

Last spring I attended a track meet at Rice University where the steeplechase was run. Midway through the steeplechase, one of the runners missed a water jump. He didn't quite clear the water pit, lost his footing, and fell headlong into the water. He lay face down in the water for what seemed an eternity. I could almost sense the struggle going on in his mind as he lay motionless in the pit: *Should I get up and keep running? Or should I stay here awhile, enjoy the cool water, and then stumble to the grass for rest? Do I really have what it takes to finish this strenuous ordeal? Or should I quit now and avoid the pain?*

Finally, he resolved the matter and splashed out of the pit. To much applause from the spectators, he gamely resumed the race. He plodded around the track and somehow managed to navigate all of the remaining water jumps. He was one of the stragglers at the finish, but he did complete the course.

That steeplechaser, lying face down in the water, needed more than additional information on steeplechase running—he needed motivation! He didn't need more strategy—he needed determination and will power! A coach shouting steeplechase techniques in his ear would have done him no good, but a coach shouting passionate words of encouragement could have benefited him greatly.

The apostle Paul frequently offered words of "technique" to early Christians. Doctrine and practical tips for living fill his letters. But Paul knew that sometimes his readers required motivation more than information. So, occasionally he shouted flaming words of exhortation to their discouraged ears. To despondent Christians, lying in the water pits of life, he often yelled, "Get up! You can do it! Keep running!"

One church that constantly needed bolstering was the church at Corinth. Corinth was an especially evil city, noted for its depravity and immorality. To be a follower of Jesus Christ in such a place was no easy task! Paul therefore wrote stirring exhortations to the Corinthian Christians in an effort to fortify their faltering faith.

The people of Corinth were familiar with athletic games, for the Isthmian Games were held every few years in their city. These games were second in size only to the Roman Olympics. The Corinthians had watched many races and had thrilled to the exploits of numerous runners. It is no surprise, then, that Paul used their knowledge of running in his motivational plea to them.

"Do you not know that in a race all the runners compete, but only one receives the prize? So run that you may obtain it," he pleaded. If you are going to run, Paul was indicating, run to win.

In *The Complete Book of Running,* James Fixx offered these words of counsel to runners who decide to enter a distance race:

> As a race continues, it's also easy to find reasons to slow down: the pain is unbearable, you tell yourself; an old injury is acting up; blisters are coming on; it isn't an impor-

tant race anyway. Such arguments can sound beguilingly
persuasive in the heat of a race. Only later, after you've
yielded to their spurious plausibility, are you disappointed
in yourself. If you're going to race at all, it's only sensible
to make a maximum effort.[1]

Those words are strangely reminiscent of the apostle's
counsel to people who had entered the Christian race.
Paul was saying, in effect, "If you're going to race at all,
it's only sensible to make a maximum effort."

But how can we do it? How can we stay motivated?
How can we keep the "fire" burning within us? Here, at
the starting line, what can we do to foster determination
and exuberance?

Paul helped answer these questions in the three verses
following his plea for us to win the race. In these verses
in the Corinthian letter, he outlined three factors which
stir up the "fire" within us and keep us motivated to live
for Christ. We can run with enthusiasm if we have (1) discipline, (2) direction, and (3) a willingness to be a pacesetter.

Discipline

In 1 Corinthians 9:25, Paul underscored the necessity of
discipline: "Every athlete exercises self-control in all
things. They do it to receive a perishable wreath, but we
an imperishable."

Any runner in the Isthmian Games who hoped to win
the coveted wreath, laid at the finish line of the race, had
to practice self-control. Self-control, or discipline, has always been indispensable to good running. Any modern
runner who wants to compete well also must be disci-
plined. The only runner who stands a chance of winning

a long race today is the one who subjects himself or herself
to rigorous training:

> Some people are easily dissuaded from running; nightfall,
> cold, heat, rain, or a few snowflakes dissolve their willpow-
> er. Yet there are few conditions under which it is impos-
> sible to run in comfort. Connecticut's winters are harsh.
> Once I ran in a blizzard so severe I could hardly push my
> door open against the wind. I was nearly blown off my feet
> on the icy roads. Yet within a few minutes, despite icicles
> on my eyebrows, I was sweating pleasantly and feeling
> fine.[2]

Running in a Connecticut blizzard? On icy roads? With
icicles on the eyebrows? It sounds absurd! But it's the
price a winner will pay.

Paul's reasoning in 1 Corinthians 9:25 is simple. If a
runner in a race will so discipline his body to win a perishable prize, how much more ought people to discipline
their lives in the Christian race! He was encouraging those
Corinthian Christians, living in a wild, undisciplined city,
to buck the tide and enter training. After all, he wrote, the
prize at the end of the race is eternal and indestructible.
Therefore, discipline your life and run to win!

The curse of our age is superficiality. I recently saw a
television commercial advertising a local radio station.
The commercial captured something significant about
our society. The commercial extoled the virtues of "light"
beer, "light" cola, "light" reading, and then the style of
music on that particular station—"light" music. "Light" is
definitely "in" these days and is far more alluring than
"heavy." Everything from our cola to our commitment is
"light," but I fear we are also becoming "light" people
with no depth.

The antidote to "light" living is discipline. Discipline

banishes superficiality and enables us to put down firm Christ-centered roots. It is no coincidence that *disciple* and *discipline* come from the same word. The two are inseparable. We cannot be disciples without discipline.

First, we must discipline our bodies. The idea that God is concerned with our souls and not our bodies is heretical. According to the Bible, God is concerned about every facet of our lives. To emphasize this to the Corinthians, Paul admonished them to honor God with their bodies:

> Do you not know that your body is a temple of the Holy Spirit within you, which you have from God? You are not your own; you were bought with a price. So glorify God in your body (1 Cor. 6:19-20).

To abuse the body is unthinkable to one who sees it as the residence of God's Spirit. We are to glorify God in our bodies. I feel that for some, losing thirty pounds in a year might be just as pleasing to God as our reading the Bible from cover to cover. And for others, starting to exercise might be just as "Christian" as starting to tithe.

Second, we must discipline our minds. Do you know the one, overriding impression non-Christians have of the church? They see it as a collection of naïve, deluded simpletons. And to our shame, their impression is often not far wrong! As followers of the brilliant Nazarene, can we be unaware, uninformed, and out of touch? Can we be content with secondhand theology passed on to us from Brother Know-It-All back home? Can we be ignorant of pressing political and social concerns? Paul himself is a prime example of one who loved God with his mind. His incisive, intellectual writings still inspire and instruct us. The more you read Paul's writings, the more you learn. It is nearly impossible to plumb his depth. Christian people ought to be the sharpest, deepest people on the face of the earth.

Third, we must discipline our spirits. The classic spiritual disciplines—prayer, study, worship, fasting, simplicity, service, and the like—are steps to a liberated, joyful life. They are the means by which we make ourselves available to God. Sadly, these life-giving disciplines are often transformed into life-draining laws. They can very easily become dreaded obligations we feel one must discharge to appease God. But these spiritual disciplines are for *our* benefit. They keep us spiritually lean in a spiritually flabby world. They give us joy because they keep us in touch with joy's Source.

Leo Tolstoy once observed, "Everybody thinks of changing humanity and nobody thinks of changing himself."[3] As we practice discipline of body, mind, and spirit, we are assuming responsibility for our lives. We are affirming that any change in humanity will have to begin with a change in self.

Direction

A second part of Paul's strategy for running to win is direction. The man or woman who will run victoriously for Christ will have a definite aim: "Well, I do not run aimlessly, I do not box as one beating the air" (1 Cor. 9:26).

Paul knew the course he was to run. There was method in his running. He wasn't shadowboxing his way through life, futilely flailing at the wind. There was purpose in how he spent his days. Couple this definite direction with intense discipline, and you have a person capable of making an impact on many others. No wonder Paul was able to accomplish so much!

The Greek word for *sin* in the New Testament literally means "to miss the mark." If sin is "missing the mark,"

surely the ultimate sin must be having no mark to aim for!
Paul is addressing that aimlessness in this verse. Anyone
who will run a winning spiritual race will have to know in
which direction to run. Anyone who will really make a
difference for Christ must have discipline hitched to definite direction.

But many people seem to lack this direction. There is
no target for their time, no discernible path for their lives.
They flit from one entertaining amusement to the next,
trying to snatch momentary joy. They move from one job
to the next anytime money beckons. They jump from one
interest to another, trying to be captivated by something.
On Thursday they'll play bridge with the Smiths; Friday
they'll go to the ball game, and Saturday they'll head to
the lake for the weekend. But there is no overarching
purpose to any of it. Like the pages of a book with no
binding, there is nothing to hold their lives together!

Paul found his life-consuming passion in Christ. He expressed it succinctly to the Philippians when he testified,
"For to me to live is Christ" (Phil. 1:21). Those words,
written from a Roman prison, spell out the singular direction of Paul's life.

When he penned those lines, there were probably
three famous men in Rome—Nero the emperor, Seneca
the philosopher, and Paul the apostle. Each lived by a
different creed.

Nero lived a life that declared, "Life is luxury." His
attempts at pleasure eventually degenerated into bawdi-
ness and profane cruelty. Selfish luxury was the aim of his
life, and he eventually committed suicide.

Seneca lived a life that affirmed, "Life is learning." He
was a brilliant philosopher, expert at argument and reason. He devoted his life to knowledge.

Paul lived a life that declared, "Life is Christ." From

prison cells and street corners, before peasants and kings, he boldly asserted that Jesus Christ offers the best hope for authentic living.

Ironically, it is the solitary voice from the Roman prison that we hear best. The emperor and the philosopher have faded into time, their influence almost nonexistent. But the apostle still moves and challenges us. His motto for living still beckons to all of us who are groping for meaning. Almost two millennia after his death, Paul's words still exalt Christ as the hope for tattered lives.

In his letter to the struggling church at Corinth, Paul summoned those Christians to remember their aim. They were not to be flighty wanderers, nibbling at the world's enticements. They were to be runners pressing resolutely for the finish line, boxers taking dead aim at the opponent. They were to attest with Paul, "To live is Christ."

In our day, when we are constantly tempted to worship Corinth's gods of money, success, sex, and pleasure, his words are remarkably appropriate. They remind us that we must make Christ our consuming passion, that we dare not flirt with false gods. They call to mind that if we are running to win, we must have direction.

Willing to Be a Pacesetter

His intense discipline and unwavering direction enabled Paul to see himself as a pacesetter in the Christian race. He was running as an example to others: "But I pommel my body and subdue it, lest after preaching to others I myself should be disqualified" (1 Cor. 9:27). He could not bear the thought of shouting encouraging words to a host of runners and then falling by the wayside himself. His discipline and direction were to enable him to practice what he preached. He wanted to be a winning participant in the race, not a disqualified bystander.

Paul later encouraged the Corinthians to "Be imitators of me, as I am of Christ" (1 Cor. 11:1). Some have suggested a touch of egotism in those words. Perhaps they are right, but those are the words of a leader, one who will step to the forefront and blaze a trail. Paul was willing to accept the responsibility and challenge of being a spiritual pacesetter for others.

This pacesetting role doesn't come easy to many of us. We see ourselves as followers rather than leaders. We would rather hide in the rear than leap to the front! Because we are by nature introverted and quiet, we shun the limelight and flee public attention.

But all of us can be positive spiritual pacesetters. Regardless of our unspectacular personalities or our feelings of inadequacy, we can still say with our lives, "Be imitators of me, as I am of Christ."

Whether or not we like it or admit it, all of us are leaders. The only person I can imagine with no leadership role is a hermit on a desolate mountain somewhere. Any of us who regularly relate to people are leaders with a surprising amount of influence.

The disgruntled housewife protests, "I just mop floors, make beds, and cook. I'm no leader!"

"Really?" I would have to reply. "Who sets the pace for the children in this home and the husband who is struggling to make a living? Who sets the pace for the neighbor who drinks coffee with you? Who leads the preschool class at Sunday school? You carry a bigger stick than you imagine!"

The single man in the apartment complex protests. "There's no way I'm a pacesetter," he scoffs. "I'm on the bottom of the totem pole at work, and I live alone. I'm no leader."

"Do you ever talk to anyone?" I would have to ask. "Do

you have family, friends, or neighbors? If so, you wield an influence over someone's life. And anytime you cast a shadow on someone, you're a leader."

Here's a little poem that hits the heart of pacesetting:

> However humble a place I may hold
> Or lowly the paths I trod,
> There's a child who bases his faith on me,
> There's a dog who thinks I am God.
>
> Lord, keep me worthy, Lord, keep me clean,
> And fearless and unbeguiled.
> Lest I lose caste in the sight of the dog,
> And the wide clear eyes of the child.
>
> Lest there come in the years to be
> The blight of a withering grief,
> And a little dog mourn for a fallen god,
> And a child for his lost belief.
>
> —C.F. Davis[4]

That poet knew that, regardless of how humble our worldly status might be, all of us cast a shadow on someone.

Even children cast shadows and set paces. One recent night I came home from the church tired and discouraged. I had gone through an unproductive day and was facing a dreaded social obligation in the evening. I wanted to crawl into bed with a cup of coffee and a good book, but I had to go out and be among a throng of people. My wife, Sherry, had also undergone a bad day, so both of us were lifeless and grumpy.

Then our ten-year-old daughter, Stacy, entered the scene. She bounced into the room and gave both of us a kiss on the cheek. She told us excitedly about her day at school. Without being asked, she began to set the table for the evening meal. We sat down to eat, and she started teaching us some new songs she had learned. That evolved into a game of "Name that Tune" around the table.

What happened was amazing. As the meal progressed, our spirits lifted. We began to laugh, name tunes, and hum melodies. By the meal's end, Sherry and I had more energy and felt we might survive the social obligation after all. We had been led out of the pit of despondency by a ten-year-old. Our daughter was the positive pacesetter in our home that night.

We can protest all we want, but the inescapable truth for all nonhermits is that we are leaders charged with influencing someone else. At home, school, work, church, or community we rub shoulders with others and carry more clout than we think.

So, we're pacesetters. The question is, What kind of pace will we set? What kind of influence will we have? Will our families know Christ, joy, and acceptance because of the pace we set? Will our classrooms move toward love and truth because of our presence there? Will our places of work be more caring, moral places because we're there? Will our churches be more alive and Christlike because we're on the rolls?

Here's a foolproof formula for personal revival. This formula has nothing to do with professional evangelists or high-powered programs. It has to do only with the inner recesses of your life. Revival will come to you when you dare to say with Paul, "I will be a pacesetter." You will experience personal spiritual renewal when you decide privately to set the pace for your family, your office, or your church. There need be no fanfare or even a public church invitation for you to come alive spiritually. You simply must determine to assume the responsibility of a pacesetter.

This formula works for churches, too. Any church anywhere that has a corps of pacesetters would experience revival. If enough individuals in a church would say, "I'll set the pace for my class, or my choir, or my outreach group," that church would perform an amazing ministry for Christ. This kind of quiet revival would, in my mind, be more effective than any preacher or program could give us. It would not be flashy or dripping with emotion, but it would be real; and it would last as long as we would be willing to insist, "Be imitators of me, as I am of Christ."

The secret to igniting personal and corporate enthusiasm is hidden in Paul's testimony to the Corinthians. He was going to "pommel" and "subdue" his body so he could set the pace for others. That's the way renewal comes. It starts as a glowing ember in one heart and then others catch fire around it. J. Wallace Hamilton expressed it well:

> Whether it's in the little church at the crossroads or the mission field in Africa or the downtown church in the great secular city, here is the key to the human heart: a touch of God in the human life that makes it radiant, until other people want what the Christian has found.[5]

You should know, as we stand poised here at the starting line, that you may find yourself one day face down in a water pit. The Christian race, as we have already seen, is fraught with hazards. No one breezes through the course trouble-free.

When you wonder whether you should rise up and keep running or merely limp off and quit, I hope you'll hear Paul's persistent voice. Before you give up on God, remember Paul's plea: "So run that you may obtain the prize." Then take a vow of discipline, reorient your direction, and start running again—this time as one bold enough to be a pacesetter.

It's time for the starter's gun. Now you know a little about the race and about some of the hurdles you must clear. You also know you are in the race to win.

I wish you Godspeed. Have a good race!

Go, . . .

The gun sounds, and the runners start quickly, jostling for inside position. But the race is a long one, and many laps must be run. Along the way, the runners will have to contend with running in the pack, the distraction of crowd noise, the possibility of fatigue and falling back, the desire for "second wind," and the need to pick up the pace. Finally, they will hear the gun signaling the final lap, and, after the race, they will claim their prizes at the winner's stand. As the race begins, each runner prays silently for victory.

4.

The Start

"I will run the way of thy commandments, when thou shalt enlarge my heart" (Ps. 119:32, KJV).

When I was in high school, a friend and I went to church visitation one Tuesday night. Our church was having a revival the next week, and we were pre-inviting people to attend those services. Our "prospect" that evening was a girl in our school whose family was in turmoil. She was also quite attractive, so our motives might have been mixed as we approached the apartment complex where she lived.

The girl's father had moved out, so only the girl, her sister, and her mother were there. They greeted us cordially and accepted our invitation with seeming delight. We left their apartment thinking they might come to our church.

Sure enough, on Sunday night they walked into the revival service. My friend and I were thrilled. Our visit had paid off! We were even more thrilled, however, when the invitation was given and the mother and two daughters came forward to declare Christ as their Lord and Saviour. They wept, embraced, and gave every indication of heartfelt repentance. One casual Tuesday night visit had resulted in three decisions for Christ!

A not-so-cheerful thing happened, though, after that night of tearful decision. As far as I remember, the mother and her daughters never were baptized and never came to our church again. That night of emotional outpouring seemingly was never translated into practical commitment.

What happened? I honestly don't know. Their decision certainly seemed genuine the night they made it. I would like to believe they later joined another church and used that decision at our church as a springboard to deeper discipleship. But I fear the worst, that their decision was all froth and no substance, and that it was somewhat less than authentic, biblical faith.

That one story, if it existed in isolation, would be a tragedy. Multiply it by thousands, and you have spiritual disaster! But that story, or a kindred version, has been repeated multitudes of times. People walk down an aisle, pray a prayer, or make a promise, but the decision never seems to take root in their lives. They start the race but quickly become disenchanted and limp off of the track.

In that same parable where Jesus described some lives as being like cluttered soil, He depicted other lives as being like shallow soil:

> And these in like manner are the ones sown upon rocky ground, who, when they hear the word, immediately receive it with joy; and they have no root in themselves, but endure for awhile; then, when tribulation or persecution arises on account of the word, immediately they fall away (Mark 4:16-17).

Shallow, "rocky" lives never really get off the starting line. Their intent is good for the moment, but no sooner has the gun sounded than they are distracted by this or that. Even in a distance race, though, a good start is vital.

The psalmist expressed well the conviction of most who begin the Christian race: "I will run the way of thy commandments, when thou shalt enlarge my heart"

(Ps. 119:32, KJV). The decision to become a Christian has two parts: a promise ("I will run the way of thy commandments") and a hope ("thou shalt enlarge my heart"). As we start the race, we pledge that we will obey God and live for Him, and then trust that He will change us, guide us, and enlarge our hearts. Every person who begins the Christian journey should begin, like the psalmist, with a promise and a hope.

Let's consider the promise in this chapter. What does it mean when we promise to run the way of God's commandments? How can we ever sort through the entirety of the Bible to know what all the commandments are? And what do we do when we discover we just can't keep all of the commandments, anyway?

Those are good questions which any serious spiritual runner should ask. If we can locate the answers, maybe we can escape a "rocky" start and begin the race with certain depth and understanding. Let's look at the commandments from three perspectives and hope these different views can help us get off to a fast start.

Moses: The Necessity of the Commandments

Can you fathom a race with no rules? No starting line? No prohibitions against pushing and shoving? No specified course for the competitors to run? That wouldn't be a race—it would be chaos! The runners would be running wildly in different directions, and the whole scene would be mass confusion.

It is fully as foolish to try to picture society, or even individual lives, without commandments. Without some basic ground rules, any society or individual life will be chaotic. God's commandments in the Bible provide men and women the guidelines and order they need to live productive, meaning-filled lives. They keep human be-

ings from running wildly in different directions, trying to
find purpose.

When God called the Israelites out of slavery in Egypt,
He gave them commandments that would provide them
needed structure. Through Moses, he gave them the prin-
ciples that would make a nation out of a motley collection
of slaves. The commandments were given to cement
these people together, enabling them to live in harmony.
These guidelines were to be the frame that held their
solitary lives together.

Eugene Peterson writes of a pastoral visit he once made
that illustrates the necessity of the commandments:

> As I entered a home to make a pastoral visit, the person
> I came to see was sitting at a window embroidering a piece
> of cloth held taut over an oval hoop. She said, "Pastor,
> while waiting for you to come I realized what's wrong with
> me—I don't have a frame. My feelings, my thoughts, my
> activities—everything is loose and sloppy. There is no bor-
> der to my life. I never know where I am. I need a frame
> for my life like this one I have for my embroidery".[1]

That woman described well the purpose of the commandments. They were to give the Israelites a border to
their lives as a nation and to keep life from becoming loose
and sloppy.

God's "ground rules" still serve to keep us from becoming too sloppy about life. They can still provide the structure we need to be purposeful, joyful people.

Take, for example, the Ten Commandments God di-
rected Moses to pass on to the Israelites. These ten princi-
ples for living outline needed structure to help us
experience what Jesus called the abundant life. Both in-
dividually and corporately we would live in confusion
without such a divine framework.

The first four Commandments structure our lives around God. If we believe there is a God, we would be fools not to include Him in our life plans. So, the Commandments tell us to build God into our days:

(1) "You shall have no other gods before me" (Ex. 20:3). God is to be the ultimate allegiance in life.
(2) "You shall not make for yourself a graven image" (v. 4). No man-made deity can compete with the Creator and Sustainer of all life.
(3) "You shall not take the name of the Lord your God in vain" (v. 7). Because God is God, He is not to be treated disrespectfully or flippantly.
(4) "Remember the sabbath day, to keep it holy" (v. 8). Weekly worship and rest from work are part of the structure humans need.

The last six Commandments provide us life-giving structure in our relationships with others. They tell us what to reverence:

(5) "Honor your father and your mother" (v. 12). We are to reverence our families.
(6) "You shall not kill" (v. 13). We are to reverence human life as a sacred image of its Creator.
(7) "You shall not commit adultery" (v. 14). We are to reverence sex as a precious gift to be handled with care.
(8) "You shall not steal" (v. 15). We are to reverence material goods and the rights of others.
(9) "You shall not bear false witness" (v. 16). We are to reverence the truth and build our lives on it.
(10) "You shall not covet" (v. 17). We are to reverence self and not feel like we constantly need more things to be of worth.

In the last chapter, I suggested that all of the classic spiritual disciplines are for our benefit. The same is true of these Commandments and all of the others in the Bible. These are not the edicts of a killjoy Deity trying to whip us into shape. The Commandments are liberating paths to meaning. God didn't set down a list of austere rules to keep us from having fun. He gave us a divine blueprint for fashioning joy! The Commandments are mapped trails that keep us from wandering into the hazardous jungle of aimless living.

One of my favorite pastimes as a boy was riding my bicycle to a local shopping center. Many times, several of us boys pedaled to the shopping center. There we tried on baseball gloves at the sporting goods store, browsed through the toys at Woolworth's, and bought some rock candy at the drugstore.

The only problem we had was the busy street en route. Bicycling along Wirt Road was a precarious endeavor and as our neighborhood grew, it became even more dangerous. Eventually we had a hard time talking our parents into our delightful jaunts to the shopping center. It looked like our bicycling adventures would be curtailed because of hazardous riding conditions.

But then a boy in our neighborhood group found a hidden path through the woods that led right to the back of the shopping center. The path was precisely wide enough for a bicycle rider to negotiate. Instead of a congested street and honking cars, we had trees, butterflies, and silence on our new trail; and the new path was a straighter, quicker shot to the center. We couldn't believe it—a way to our goal free of hassle and headache. From the time we discovered the "back trail," we never again rode the longer, dangerous route.

I have come to see God's commandments as a sort of

"back trail" to our goal of purposeful living. Through His Word, He has presented a way to avoid much of the confusion and struggle of being human. Without His help, we would have to hunt for workable trails on our own. With His help, we have an invaluable Trail Guide who promises a better adventure if we'll try life His Way. Perhaps the Bible would be more intriguing to us if we saw it as a hidden path to joy, awaiting discovery by any willing explorer.

Our promise to run the route of the commandments, then, is not one we have to make with dread. We're not yielding to a tyrant; we're submitting to One who loves us and wants us to experience all that life has to offer.

That's why He gave us the commandments in the first place—to keep us from having to grope blindly through life. He gave us some rules for abundant living—a "frame"—because we need structure and direction.

Jesus: The Essence of the Commandments

If there were only Ten Commandments, we might stand a chance of obeying them. But the Bible is brimming with divine injunctions. We can't even count the commandments, much less keep them! By the time of Jesus, the rabbis had counted 613 commandments, both biblical and extra-biblical—365 negative and 248 positive. To make matters even more complicated, there were a multitude of interpretations of these divine mandates. Then there were interpretations of the interpretations!

What was intended to be a blessing of needed structure for human life had degenerated into a burden of trivial laws. Structured joy was replaced by silly nit-picking. Glad obedience had become rigid bookkeeping.

This approach to the commandments naturally produced some strange people! Some of the most "religious"

people in Jesus' day were legalists trying to keep the letter
of the law while neglecting its spirit. Even a casual reading of the New Testament will show you what Jesus
thought of this jot-and-tittle approach to religion.

In the Jewish Talmud, there is a listing of the seven
kinds of Pharisees in New Testament times. The list will
show you that silliness sometimes masquerades as piety.
The seven kinds of Pharisees were:

(1) Shechemites—who keep the law for what it will
profit them.

(2) Tumblers—always hanging down the head and dragging the feet.

(3) Bleeders—who, to avoid looking at women, close
their eyes and so bump their heads.

(4) Mortars—who covered their eyes with a cap in the
form of a mortar.

(5) What-Am-I-Yet-to-Doers—who, as soon as one law is
kept, ask what is next.

(6) Fearers—who keep the law from a fear of judgment.

(7) Lovers—who obey God because they love Him with
all the heart.[2]

Obviously, God's intent for mankind had become ob-
scured by religious silliness! By the time of Jesus, much
extraneous sludge had accumulated. Through the years,
the dust of man's error had settled over God's diamond
and dimmed its brilliance. The purpose of the commandments had been lost, even (or especially!) by the religious
elite.

That is why we owe a debt of gratitude to an unnamed
scribe who one day asked Jesus a question: "Teacher,
which is the great commandment in the law?" (Matt. 22:-
36). That query gave Jesus an opportunity to distill all the
commandments down to their essence:

And he said to him, "You shall love the Lord your God
with all your heart, and with all your soul, and with all your
mind. This is the great and first commandment. And a
second is like it, You shall love your neighbor as yourself.
On these two commandments depend all the law and the
prophets" (vv. 37-40).

The commandments, crystallized to their ultimate
meaning, are summed up by the word "love." The condensed commandments, according to Jesus, are, first, love
God with everything you have and are and, second, love
others as you love yourself. Those two declarations sum up
all of the law and prophets.

For those of us who sometimes become confused by all
of the commandments in the Bible, here's a straightfor-
ward, simple guide. To those who have ever gotten
bogged down trying to wade through Leviticus and
Deuteronomy, here's a three-verse commentary by the
Master Teacher that explains it all. Love God and love
people!

You don't need an advanced degree in theology to comprehend that! Here's an easily-read compass by which we
can steer our lives. We are to love! Running the way of the
commandments means we make a promise to love God
and to love others.

How easy it is, though, to forget the heart of our promise to God. Our religion can very easily degenerate just
like that of the New Testament Pharisees. We may come
to see the essence of our calling as knowing theology,
attending church, damning sin, or having the correct
view of Christ's second coming. All of those are important, but they are not the heartbeat of the Christian calling. At its core, Christianity centers in love.

So, we probably owe that nameless scribe more than we
realize. His question provided Jesus with the opportunity

to crystallize the commandments. Now anyone can understand their essence: The commandments are about love.

Paul: The Futility of Keeping the Commandments

There's still a fly in the ointment, though. We have been able to condense all of the law and prophets down to manageable size—love God and love people. But knowing we are to love and actually loving are two different matters! And the sad truth is that all of us are miserable failures at love. Our love placed alongside Jesus' love is an embarrassment. Yes, we are supposed to love, but pulling it off doesn't come easy.

"But wait!" some righteous person says. "Speak for yourself. I do a fine job of keeping the commandments. I love God. I have a loving family. I don't believe in violence, and I've never been unfaithful to my spouse. Don't tell me I don't love or keep God's commandments!"

Really? Try Jesus' interpretation of the commandments on for size. Anger without a cause, not just murder, is a violation of the commandments. Lust, not just adultery, is a trespass of God's laws. Love not just your family and friends but stretch that love to cover even your enemies. His Way includes turning the other cheek, giving away your coat, and going the second mile. Jesus looks behind our action and examines our attitude. On our good days, we might be able to keep the letter of the law, but how many of us have the pure, selfless spirit Jesus demands? If one thinks he can live the Way Jesus describes, he doesn't understand what He asks of us!

No, even the most righteous of us cannot keep the commandments. On our finest, holiest days we fall far short of God's ideal. Even when we appear outwardly clean to our friends, we know we are contaminated inside.

So we seem to be trapped. We are led to keep the commandments, but none of us can do it. Like the psalmist, when we try to run the way of the commandments, we find our effort to be futile. We discover ourselves wailing with Isaiah: "Woe is me! For I am lost; for I am a man of unclean lips, and I dwell in the midst of a people with unclean lips" (Isa. 6:5). We end up on our knees confessing with David: "For I know my transgressions, and my sin is ever before me" (Ps. 51:3). We find ourselves concluding with Paul: "For all have sinned and fall short of the glory of God" (Rom. 3:23).

In the Galatian letter, Paul used two interesting illustrations to describe our plight. First, we are in jail to our inability to keep God's laws: "Now before faith came, we were confined under the law, kept under restraint until faith should be revealed" (Gal. 3:23). The law, Paul explained, is like a jail, and it's impossible to break out! Second, the law is like a custodian, or schoolmaster, to us: "So that the law was our custodian until Christ came, that we might be justified by faith" (v. 24). The law also serves as a stern teacher with exacting standards.

But notice the purpose of the commandments in these verses. The law kept us under restraint *until faith should be revealed.* The law served as our custodian *until Christ came.* Our futility in keeping the commandments leads us to a Savior: "For in Christ Jesus you are all sons of God, through faith" (Gal. 3:26). The commandments usher us into the presence of a crucified Christ.

This is the good news of the gospel—our futility forces us to find a Savior! Since we cannot pass the test, we must locate One who can pass it for us. When we trust Christ, we are admitting our failure and accepting His gift. Our admission that we cannot measure up to God's ideal opens the door to the salvation Christ purchased for us on the cross. We accept the gift and spend the rest of our days celebrating it.

When we can say with Paul, "I am the foremost of sinners" (1 Tim. 1:15), then we can also exult with him:

> There is therefore now no condemnation for those who are in Christ Jesus. For the law of the Spirit of life in Christ Jesus has set me free from the law of sin and death (Rom. 8:1-2).

When we acknowledge that the commandments are just too much for us, we can then sing with the apostle:

> where sin increased, grace abounded all the more, so that, as sin reigned in death, grace also might reign through righteousness to eternal life through Jesus Christ our Lord (Rom. 5:20-21).

This, then, is the surprising good news about our predicament: Though we cannot pass God's test, we are to live our lives celebrating the fact that Jesus has already passed it for us. Our frustration is transformed into freedom. Our futile works are transformed into glad acceptance of His grace.

These three perspectives on the commandments can send us off to a good start. They help us grasp the meaning of our promise to live for God, to run the Way of His commandments.

The commandments, from Moses' perspective, offer us needed structure and guidance. Without them, the race would be aimless and confusing.

Jesus' perspective offers us a crystallizing word that sharpens our understanding. The essence of our promise is a commitment to love God and love people.

Paul's perspective gives us a message of grace. He helps

us see that the commandments are not a stepladder to God, that only faith in Christ will save us. Paul's celebrative statement rescues us from despair.

So we're off and running! We've made our pledge to run God's Way. Now, we're hoping that as we run, he will "enlarge our hearts." And we await the unseen challenges we still must face.

Here is one final word of strategy for beginning the Christian race. It comes from an Olympic marathoner from England who was asked his secret of success. His reply? "I start at a brisk pace and run at ever-increasing speeds."

Now that's a winning strategy—one I wish the mother and her two daughters at our revival had adopted.

May your start be brisk and your speeds ever-increasing!

5.

Running in the Pack

"Again I saw that under the sun the race is not to the swift,
nor the battle to the strong, nor bread to the wise, nor
riches to the intelligent, nor favor to the men of skill; but
time and chance happen to them all" (*Eccl. 9:11*).

Indelibly etched in my memory is that awful Zola
Budd-Mary Decker collision in the 1984 Summer Olympics. They were running at the front of a tightly-bunched
pack in the three thousand meters when they became
entangled. Mary stumbled and fell on the infield by the
track, her pain, disappointment, and frustration obvious
to millions who watched around the world. Zola continued to run, but, shocked and disheartened, she was
nowhere near the leaders at the finish.

Some observers were quick to point accusing fingers:
"Zola cut in too quickly. Her inexperience was evident."
Or "Mary should have known better than to get trapped
in the inside lane. She shouldn't have allowed herself to
be boxed in like that."

Others adopted the impartial approach to the mishap:
"It was no one's fault. Jostling in a tight pack of runners
is always a hazardous situation. Any runner could get tangled or bumped and meet disaster. Such is life when
you're running in the pack."

I found myself unwilling to throw stones at either runner. It was a sad, tragic incident that destroyed years of
training and dreaming. Both Zola and Mary will grieve for
years over their collision; and I, in a small way, grieve with
them over their shattered dream. Yet, I believe the im-

partial view is best: Put the blame on no one. Know that every race has built-in hazards. Recognize the danger of running in the pack.

One man who understood that danger lived centuries BC. He is known biblically as "Qoheleth," the Preacher who wrote the Book of Ecclesiastes. His ancient words sound like a modern commentary on the Budd-Decker mishap: "Again I saw that under the sun the race is not to the swift . . . but time and chance happen to them all" (Eccl. 9:11). The Preacher knew that jostling in the pack is bad business, that "time" and "chance" can send even the swiftest runners sprawling.

Some have wondered, upon reading the Book of Ecclesiastes, why the Preacher's words ever made it into Scripture. Ecclesiastes appears to be a negative, pessimistic book, chockfull of the ominous Hebrew word *hebel.* The word is usually translated *vanity* and describes a life that is fraudulent, superficial, and empty. The word is used more in Ecclesiastes than in all of the rest of the Old Testament. The Preacher is cynical because he sees that so much of life is *hebel,* a cotton-candy existence, void of meaning. He wrote his book to counter this vain, flighty approach to life.

Qoheleth was a tell-it-like-it-is preacher, intent on destroying an empty piety that looked like genuine faith:

> In the same way that the Psalms are an appropriate conclusion to the New Testament, Ecclesiastes is an appropriate introduction. People bring so many mistaken expectations to the gospel, so much silly sentiment, and so many petulant demands, that they hardly hear its real message or confront its actual promise. Qoheleth gets rid of all that. He empties us of the inner noise that we supposed was religion and the cluttered piety we supposed

was faith. He throws out the accumulated religious junk
and banishes the fraud that has paraded as faith.[1]

To all of us who desire "the real thing" spiritually, the
Preacher has several pithy points to make.

And one of those points is that we are running in the
human pack. Our trust in God, according to the Preacher,
does not guarantee us a life on "Easy Street." Neither does
our serving God exempt us from our humanity. We are
still human and will have to struggle with sin and sorrow
like other humans. And "time" and "chance" will happen
to us all.

Let us probe further into what it means to live with
"time" and "chance," and try to develop a strategy for
successfully running in the pack.

Relentless Time

Like others in the pack, we will have to deal with relentless time. It continually stalks us, even though we try
our best to avoid it. We try to run from time with our hair
dyes, fitness programs, face-lifts, and "with-it" clothes, but
we will not escape it. Time eventually catches up with
everyone.

Early in life, it seems that we chase time. We yearn to
grow older, for time to move. We long for birthdays, so we
can be more grown-up, so we can go on dates, so we can
drive a car.

But somewhere along the race, the tables turn. Suddenly time starts chasing us. We feel pursued by something that puts wrinkles on our faces and aches in our
joints. We wish time would leave us alone. We try to flee
its relentless hounding, but we constantly feel it breathing
down our necks. Like the Preacher observed, time hap-

pens to all of us, and we must know how to handle it if we are to keep from stumbling.

How do we deal with relentless time? What kind of strategy can we employ to keep from tripping over the ever-present clock? Here are three declarations that can help.

Declaration One: I will use time, and not let time use me.

The clock is a bully. It will push you around if you let it. It will tell you when to eat, sleep, work, worship, and play. It will actually call all the shots if you give in to it. Rather than using time, you will discover that time is using you.

Our nation is definitely time conscious, and most of us have a serious case of "hurry sickness." We're always checking clocks, glancing at watches, listening for hourly "beeps," and writing engagements on our calendars. We have no flexibility or freedom because we're tyrannized by time. Notice sometime how unhurried Jesus always seems to be in the Gospels. He gives no impression of a busy crusader with a complex agenda for each day. He always seemed to have time for people, time to stop and talk, time for parties with tax collectors, time to fish with the disciples. But when we look at ourselves, we don't find that relaxed flexibility. Our lives are programmed by the clock.

We must begin asking not "What time is it?" but "What is it time *for?*" What should we be doing to make our lives useful and meaningful and to enrich our relationships? How shall we find joy? Robert Capon, himself a recreational runner, made this telling observation in his book, *A Second Day:*

There's no point, for example, in trying to go running at

5:30 A.M. in January. There are no street lights: it's so dark you could—and I almost did—break an ankle. Once I realized that, I gave up setting alarms and got up with the light instead.

I shifted, in other words, from the habit of asking what time it was to the saner procedure of asking what it was time for. When that sank in as far as running was concerned, I decided to apply it to the rest of what goes on here as well. The way we arrange a day is to determine what jobs need doing and set an order for doing them. Then we follow the order till they're finished and go to bed. I recommend the arrangement. It's not only productive; the best thing about it is that it gets things done without letting them ride roughshod over the human beings involved.[2]

I know we are all hemmed in by job schedules and other pressing commitments. We cannot throw away our clocks and calendars and disregard time (except perhaps on Saturdays and vacations!). But neither do we have to be enslaved by an unyielding schedule that is always pushing and pressing us into joyless busyness. We can choose to look at the clock less, to ask what it is time *for* in our lives, and to use time instead of letting it use us.

Declaration Two: I will measure time by its quality, not quantity.

In many ways, the Greek language used in the New Testament surpasses our modern English language. The New Testament Greek, for instance, has three words for *love.* We have to use the same word *love* to describe how we feel about our spouse and what we think about chocolate pie. The Greek, with three words for *love,* is more precise and descriptive.

The Greek language also has two words for our word

time. There is *chronos,* which is clock time and measures quantity. But there is also *kairos,* which is real, experiential time and measures quality. When we say, "It's time for the party," we're using time as *chronos.* When we get home from the party and say, "I had the time of my life," we're talking about *kairos.*

That Greek distinction is most helpful. Our goal, I think, is to have more *kairos* in our lives, to spend our days in experiences and relationships that have true quality. We all have twenty-four hours of *chronos* each day, but we each determine for ourselves how much *kairos* we will have.

Our battle, then, is not simply with advancing years (*chronos*) but with boredom and lifelessness (*kairos*). Runner-philosopher George Sheehan spoke of this battle when he wrote, "The fight, then, is never with age; it is with boredom, with routine, with the danger of not living at all. Then life will stop, growth will cease, learning will come to an end. You no longer become who you are. You begin to kill time or live it without thought or purpose."[3]

When we get to that point, we have *chronos* but no *kairos.* We have nothing that enables us to savor life, that gives us joy. So, we should begin now to think of time as *kairos,* as quality experiences. We need to find people, books, hobbies, ministries, and a relationship with God that will allow us to really *live* while we're alive.

Declaration Three: I will dare to believe in life beyond time.

Even the somewhat pessimistic Preacher knew this: "[God] has put eternity into man's mind" (Eccl. 3:11). He knew that mankind was made in the image of the eternal God and that we have a "homing instinct" that points beyond time.

A contemporary writer, Peter Kreeft, echoed the

Preacher's sentiments in his book, *Heaven, the Heart's Deepest Longing:*

> We have a homing instinct, a "home detector," and it doesn't ring for earth. That's why nearly every society in history except our own instinctively believes in life after death. Like the great mythic wanderers, like Ulysses and Aeneas, we have been trying to get home. Earth just doesn't smell like home. However good a road it is, however good a motel it is, however good a training camp it is, it is not home. Heaven is.[4]

Those of us who know about the cross and resurrection realize that in those events God transcended time. He came as one of us, died a horrible, unjustified death, but then miraculously rose again to prove that time could not hold Him in its clutches. And the promise that we cling to is that we, too, will one day transcend time. Yes, we will grow old. Yes, our skin will wrinkle. Yes, our muscles will wither. And yes, we will die. But we will not lose our contest with time. We, too, will burst through time's limitations into an eternity with a Father who loves us.

The apostle Paul one day looked death and time squarely in the face and spoke for all of us who follow Jesus when he exulted, "Thanks be to God who gives us the victory through our Lord Jesus Christ" (1 Cor. 15:57).

Impartial Events

The Preacher also indicated we will have to deal with "chance" as we run in the pack. By "chance" I think he is referring to what an unknown sage has called "life's appalling impartiality." We will be forced to contend with some unpredictable, undeserved, unwanted circumstances.

Ten years ago, we stood with our best friends at the

graveside of their baby daughter. Our first children had arrived just months apart—ours was a healthy girl; theirs was a beautiful child but born with a serious heart defect. She lived eleven difficult months and died.

To this day, I cannot explain or justify her death. We didn't deserve a perfectly-formed child because we were good, and our friends certainly didn't deserve a baby with heart problems because they were bad. All we could do at the cemetery was grieve and shake our heads in mystery at life's impartiality. Jesus stated that it rains on the just and the unjust, and that sad day it rained sorrow on the just.

I was not the first to wonder about those perplexing matters. The Preacher knew about this and spoke of it:

> For man does not know his time. Like fish which are taken in an evil net, and like birds which are caught in a snare, so the sons of men are snared at an evil time, when it suddenly falls upon them (Eccl. 9:12).

Job, Jeremiah, David, Jonah, and John the Baptist are other people of faith who struggled in Scripture with life's appalling impartiality.

A few years ago, Rabbi Harold Kushner wrote *When Bad Things Happen to Good People.* The book stayed on the best-seller list for months, bearing eloquent testimony that modern people still struggle with evil and suffering. We still would like to know why the rain seemingly falls at random. Philip Yancey has written, "How can a good God permit a suffering world? is the perennial question rustling through the pages of theology."[5] It is also the perennial question rustling through our minds.

So, what do we do when we face life's impartiality, when we stare into the hollow eyes of suffering? Again, I think there are sure declarations that can help us in such situations. Perhaps we will never have all of the answers we want, but I believe these assertions can help us better cope with impartial events.

Declaration One: I will ask the right questions.

It is easy to become mired in the "whys": Why is this happening to me? Why did God do this thing? Why don't my friends understand? Why doesn't God rescue me from this misery? Such questions are inevitable, and at times we need to join our biblical forefathers in asking "why."

But we shouldn't linger there too long. Most of those "why" questions are speculative and philosophical, and they don't yield answers. Mystery often reigns supreme, and we can go crazy trying to make life fit together neatly like a jigsaw puzzle.

Ultimately, "what" and "how" are better questions for unsticking us from "chance": What should I do now? What is my best alternative in this less-than-ideal circumstance? What can I learn from this experience? How can I turn this into victory? How can I glorify God in this situation? How can I serve others in spite of this problem?

Those questions can yield practical, productive answers that can keep us out of the mire. They are not always easy to ask, because "why" keeps coming to our lips. But "what" and "how" can cause us to move again, can remind us that life is for living, not speculating. When confronted with circumstances we cannot understand, we can still ask the right questions.

Declaration Two: I will accept God's help, however it comes.

We have pretty well limited God's help to what I call "mechanical help." We believe God is helping us when He "fixes things up," rescues us from a sticky situation, or miraculously alters the normal course of events. When we pray for God's assistance, it is nearly always this mechanical kind of help we have in mind.

But God often gives us "personal help." He may not always dissolve the tumor or remove the job pressure, but He promises to join with us in our pain, to give strength and hope, and to love us no matter what. We should never underestimate this personal help God gives:

> When we are helpless, there he is. He doesn't start your stalled car for you; he comes and sits with you in the snowbank. You can object that he should have made a world in which cars don't stall; but you can't complain he doesn't stick by his customers.[6]

Think of Jesus seeking God's help in the garden of Gethsemane. He earnestly prayed that the cup would pass, that God would remove the cross from His future. But it was not to be. He died in agony between two thieves.

Was the Father deaf to Jesus' plea? I think not. He certainly did not give Him "mechanical help" and rescue Him from death. But God did provide "personal help." He gave Him peace in the face of awesome pressure and love in the midst of unthinkable cruelty. Make no mistake: God heard and answered His Son's cry.

And I trust that He hears ours, too. We always want "mechanical help," but sometimes the gift given is His presence, His personal help. An essential part of dealing with life's suffering is to accept His help in whatever form it comes.

Declaration Three: I will trust the character of God.

I once read about a man who wrote a book concerning women. Some years later, when he came to know more about them, he republished his book. But rather than revising all the material, he wrote this blanket correction in the preface:

> Wherever in this volume appears the word "is," substitute "is not"—and wherever the words "is not" appear, substitute "maybe," "perhaps," or "God knows."[7]

There is, to be sure, a great amount of unpredictability and inconsistency in all of us—men and women alike. But God is utterly dependable. Way back in the Book of Genesis, Abraham, when confronted with a situation he could not comprehend, asked, "Shall not the Judge of all the earth do right?" (Gen. 18:25). The answer that resounds through Scripture is a definite "Yes!" We can rest our lives, our hurts, and our unanswerable questions on the character of God. He will do right.

Because we trust in the goodness of God, we do not despair in the presence of the Preacher's "chance." Things will happen that are unfair and impossible to explain, but we hold firmly to the conviction that God will ultimately do right. Our hope is not in our understanding, but in One whose character is unshakably righteous.

John Kennedy Toole, a young novelist, tried for years to locate a publisher for his manuscript. None would accept it, and he sank into a depression that eventually led to suicide. Several years after his death, his mother bundled up his manuscript and set out to find a publisher. Eventually she succeeded. No one could have guessed the book's good fortune. *A Confederacy of Dunces* became a bestseller and won the Pulitzer Prize. How tragic that the author despaired before he saw his dream fulfilled. If there is a moral to his life, it is surely this: Don't give up before the final curtain is drawn.

We who trust the character of God must not despair

before the curtain of history is brought down. We will face evil, be humbled by life's injustices, and shake our heads in disbelief at life's appalling impartiality. But we will not abandon hope, because we believe the God of love is in full control of His creation. We will run the race with patience because we believe so strongly in the Judge at the finish line.

There is an old adage, "To be forewarned is to be forearmed." The Preacher forewarned us in the verse in Ecclesiastes that we are running in the pack. We will have to jostle with "time" and "chance" like others. But we can "forearm" ourselves against disaster. We do not have to take a spill if we know how to cope with these inevitable nemeses. We can learn to run with confidence, and we can avoid the tumble that can occur so easily when we run in the pack.

6.
Crowd Noise

"Therefore, since we are surrounded by so great a crowd of witnesses . . ." (*Heb. 12:1a*).

The writer of Hebrews pictured in this verse a vast arena full of spectators cheering a runner to victory. The image of Joan Benoit entering the roaring stadium at the end of her Olympic Marathon comes to mind when I read this verse. Certainly the Christian race would be easier to run if we had a host of such supportive witnesses rooting us on.

But what about the other possibility? What about crowd noise that distracts and confuses? What about the possibility of crowd racket that destroys our concentration and throws us off course? What about the jangling sounds in our culture that keep us from hearing "the still, small voice"? To this more sinister kind of crowd noise we turn our attention in this chapter.

The races I run are not known for their crowd noise—at least not when *I* cross the finish line. The leaders no doubt hear a few yells and receive some crowd encouragement, but I'm never close enough to hear it. Nor am I usually at the tail end of the pack to hear the sympathetic applause that comes to those who feel victorious just to finish. I'm usually in the middle somewhere, jogging along in sweaty obscurity. In some races, my wife and two children will offer support and assure me I'm looking great—even though I look like I'm one step away from total collapse.

But usually I cross the line to no one's congratulations but my own.

On the other end of the spectrum, I've never experienced negative crowd reaction, either. I have never been booed, laughed at, or heckled. I *have* been chased and nipped by dogs. I *have* dodged cars on busy streets. I *have* sweated in hot, humid summers and frozen in icy winters, but I have never had a problem with people. They either smile as I glide by or ignore me as "just another crazy jogger."

Not all runners are so fortunate. The late Jim Fixx, in *The Complete Book of Running,* offered a few suggestions to those who face hecklers. There are, he said, three approaches: (1) ignore the troublemakers, (2) fight back, or (3) smile and be friendly (heap coals of fire on their heads!).

He told of one runner who chose to fight back. This particular runner had been heckled and bothered by a car full of teenagers. When their car stopped at a traffic light, he embarked on a newly-devised path. He took three strides—one on the trunk, one on the top, and one on the hood—leaving three dents to mark his passage!

Most runners will not (and should not) be so bold, but I suppose it is smart to know how to handle hecklers should the need arise.

And those of us trying to live for Christ in an unchristian world need to have a strategy for dealing with negative crowd noise, too. Two questions, specifically, must be asked: (1) Can I even recognize distracting crowd noise when I hear it? and (2) If so, what will I do about it?

I can think of no better place for solid answers to those questions than the book of 1 John. Written to early Christians being distracted by crowd noise, John's book is a call to spurn false faith and cling to real. John had many definite points to make about the "noise" that was pulling first-century saints away from Christ. His words to ancient "runners" still ring true to those of us wanting to stay on course.

"Outside" Noise

The raucous sounds of secularism are not new. Even in the first century, those outside the community of faith were shouting so loudly they threatened to drown the gospel tune. John confronted this "outside" noise in his First Epistle and made some blunt assertions:

> Do not love the world or the things in the world. If any one loves the world, love for the Father is not in him. For all that is in the world, the lust of the flesh and the lust of the eyes and the pride of life, is not of the Father but is of the world. And the world passes away and the lust of it; but he who does the will of God abides for ever (1 John 2:15-17).

When John used the word "world," he was not referring to God's created order. Obviously, we are to love that world and be stewards of its magnificent treasures. No, "world" in this passage referred to life apart from God, a "worldly" mind-set contrary to the ways of the Spirit.

The fatal flaw in the world's citizens is an obsessive preoccupation with self. In the "world," self is god. The three sins John pinpointed in this passage highlight this selfishness. Let us place them under a mental microscope for a moment so we can see the characteristics of the "world."

The Lust of the Flesh

The first characteristic of those in the world is "the lust of the flesh." This phrase describes one whose life is dominated by the pleasure principle. Its creed is, "If it feels good, do it." Anyone afflicted with "the lust of the flesh" eagerly bows before the triune deity whose names are Luxury, Pleasure, and Possessions. In paying homage to these secular gods, such old-fashioned concepts as discipline, sacrifice, and spiritual conviction are junked as religious relics.

"Seek first your own welfare, and all these things shall be yours as well," say those in the world. But Jesus saw it differently: "Seek first his kingdom and his righteousness, and all these things shall be yours as well" (Matt. 6:33). It's all a matter of where we choose to focus our love.

The Lust of the Eyes

This second characteristic of the world's citizens describes an infatuation with externals. Anyone with "the lust of the eyes" is enamored with tinsel and bangles. Showiness and impressiveness are all-important. "The lust of the eyes" makes us ask a whole flock of life-and-death questions: What will this do to my image? Is this the "in" thing to do? Am I eating at the fancy places? How did I "come across" in that conversation? Is this the right label for me to wear to appear "chic"?

Such questions cause us to focus on the externals to the exclusion of internals. Paul told the Corinthians that his outer man was decaying, but his inner man was being renewed every day. Sadly, for those with "the lust of the eyes," the outer man (despite their frantic efforts) is decaying, and the inner man is, too. Not so with the Christian.

The Pride of Life

This third characteristic is similar to "the lust of the eyes" in that it makes impressing others life's goal. The Pharisee on the street corner, intoning his eloquent "prayer" for all passersby to hear, had a typical case of "the pride of life." This worldly sin puffs a person up with unhealthy, crowd-oriented ego. The ones with this affliction always have one eye cocked to the masses for signs of approval.

Actually, "the pride of life" is normal ego gone to seed. It is healthy and normal to want to please others, to yearn for approval. Without that quality, our world would be a chaotic place of devil-may-care individualists. The desire to "fit in" is good, but "the pride of life" takes that good desire and stretches it too far. It makes us human chameleons, ready to change colors at a moment's notice. It lets other people set our agenda—where we eat, what we drive, what we wear, who we befriend. When we do anything for a token of the world's acceptance, we have been ensnared by "the pride of life."

In light of these three glaring flaws, John's counsel was pointed: "Do not love the world or the things in the world" (1 John 2:15).

In other words, "Don't let the discordant tones of 'outside' noise drown the smooth harmony you have learned in Christ." John wanted those early Christians to listen beneath the blaring sounds of secularity for another rhythm—a rhythm that could really lead them to joy.

It was true in John's day and in ours: Appearances are deceiving. What looks like nourishment turns out to be cotton candy. What looks like genuine fun turns out to be the joy-sapping "lust of the flesh." What looks like true excitement turns out to be the cheap "lust of the eyes." What looks like friendship turns out to be the self-serving "pride of life." What we think we see is all too often not what we get.

That is a lesson I have learned, too, in the races I have run. Show me a runner who looks fancy—new shoes, expensive garb, complicated watch—and I will show you a runner I can probably beat. Show me a runner who looks like a garage-sale refugee—dilapidated shoes, faded shorts, gaunt as a buzzard—and I will show you a runner who will be through and sipping a soft drink when I finish. I learned it early in my running career: Look beneath the facade.

That, I think, was John's point to the distracted Christians in the early church. He was counseling them not to be sidetracked by the alluring temptations of the world, not to be tricked by appearances. He didn't want them to be thrown off course by the sounds of "outside" crowd noise.

"Inside" Noise"

Those early Christians also had to contend with "inside" noise as they tried to run the race. Much of 1 John has as its backdrop the Gnostic heresy. Gnosticism was a system of religious thought that accentuated knowledge. The Gnostics had special, "elitist" ceremonies and saw themselves as possessors of unique truth. Among other things, these "super-spiritual" people denied the humanity of Christ and believed anything material was inherently evil.

But Gnosticism came from within the Christian community: "They went out from us, but they were not of us; for if they had been of us, they would have continued with us; but they went out, that it might be plain that they all are not of us" (1 John 2:19). John certainly saw the Gnostic way as falsehood and boldly stated one of his main purposes for penning his letter: "I write this to you about those who would deceive you" (v. 26).

Because Gnosticism grew from within the church, it was a more subtle deception than the obvious rattling rhythm of the world. After all, the Gnostics were spiritual people! They worshiped, prayed, quoted Scripture, and were excited about their faith. What could be wrong with that?

Everything! Some of the worst evil in history has presented itself as ardent faith. Not everyone who quotes Scripture is Christlike, not everyone who frequents the church house knows about love, and not every system that carries the Christian banner is, in truth, Christian.

Even today we must be alert to "inside" noises that would destroy our witness or rain on our joy. Gnosticism as a system vanished centuries ago, but less-than-biblical systems still flourish. And because those inadequate systems look and sound so "spiritual," they are probably more devastating than noises from the outside.

In particular, let me mention four "inside," religious noises that clamor for our attention today.

Loveless Legalism

This approach to Christianity emphasizes rules to the exclusion of love. As we have already seen, love is the very heartbeat of the Christian Way, but loveless legalism overlooks love in a strained attempt to keep rules. The Pharisees whom Jesus rebuked so harshly were classic examples of people who detached law from love.

This way of approaching Christianity is seductive because it appears so biblical. Loveless legalism says, "Know Scripture," and we all should. It says, "Be righteous," and we all should be. It says, "Obedience is crucial," and that is a message we all need to hear. Who can deny the validity of many of the legalist's claims?

But in separating law from love, the legalists have a cold, doctrinal system that is far removed from the tender touch of the Carpenter. And loveless legalism tends to become bogged down in minute details. It examines the bark on the trees but is blind to the forest. It knows laws and interpretations of laws, but it doesn't know how to give a cup of cold water in Jesus' name.

Because Gnosticism was like Pharisaism in its emphasis on doctrine, John wrote much in his epistle about the priority of love. And because loveless legalism is alive and well in our country today, we must remind ourselves again and again that "love is of God, and he who loves is born of God and knows God. He who does not love does not know God; for God is love" (1 John 4:7-8).

Graceless Activism

Loveless legalism is law separated from love; graceless activism is works detached from grace. It preaches all of the right things—obedience, sacrifice, selflessness, and all of the spiritual disciplines—but it has one tragic shortcoming: Its motivation is wrong.

Graceless activism is motivated by obligation instead of grace. It says, "I will keep the commandments to prove my devotion to God. I will try my hardest to be a dedicated disciple. I will impress God, the world, and myself with my sainthood." Those are noble goals, all right, but they quickly degenerate into burdensome religion. Spiritual activity apart from grace always leads to disillusionment. Graceless activists eventually "run down" and "burn out." The follower of Christ can only run so far without a fresh reminder of the wonder of God's grace.

Marathoners speak of "hitting the wall" when they run. About twenty miles into a marathon, the body is often totally depleted, and runners find it impossible to continue. The body literally shuts down and will not function. Who will ever forget that wrenching last-lap struggle of Swiss marathoner Gabriela Andersen-Scheisse in the 1984

Olympics? Her pace slowed to a swerving stumble and her body was completely out of control. She was a grim picture of the agony of "hitting the wall." Many a game runner has failed to finish the twenty-six mile course because of that dreaded "wall."

Christians who run too long without the rejuvenation of grace "hit the wall," too. The Christian life becomes a laborious struggle, an exhausting effort to carry on, even though all energy is spent. There is no telling how many faithful church folks have "hit the wall" and lost all joy in the race. Activism without grace is as deadly in the spiritual race as marathoning without water stops is in the physical one.

All graceless activists need to memorize 1 John 4:19: "We love, because he first loved us." *First,* it says, He loved us—not because we're good, devoted, or attend church even on Sunday night. No, He loved us before any of our works. That, gloriously, is grace. We are the apple of God's eye! All of our efforts are not to earn that love but to show our gratitude for it. We love, worship, pray, and do all other spiritual activities because He loved us first.

Artless Pragmatism

Pragmatism is the philosophical king of our day. It is concerned only with results and steadfastly declares, "If it works, do it." And we who have pledged our lives to Christ are not immune to its tempting noises. We certainly want results, so we blithely join in singing the popular chorus that goes, "The ends justify the means. Do whatever works."

Virginia Stem Owens wrote,

The only question admitted as valid by a pragmatist is "does it work?" Yet never before have we so desperately needed some guide, some scale of judgment for determining, on grounds other than pragmatism, what is fitting and proper, in the original sense of that word, to an expression of the Christian faith. For at least the past few decades all the forms of our expression have been borrowed, even stolen, from our surrounding milieu, and that very uncritically. The results have been ridiculous, absurd, and sometimes heretical.[1]

We in the Christian tradition come from a long line of people who recognize the importance of style. "How" a book is written, or a song composed, or a sermon preached, or a picture painted *is* important. Ours is the heritage of the lyrically moving psalms, the fierce but poetic prophets, the delightful parables of Jesus, the brilliant letters of Paul. Our heritage is not one of pragmatism, but of artistic style and concentration on craftsmanship.

Elton Trueblood once warned, "Holy shoddy is still shoddy."[2] We must not be guilty of shoddy discipleship in any area. Let the preacher wrestle for exactly the right word to paint his verbal picture. Let the Sunday school teacher view her work in the fourth-grade department as a craft. Let the music man polish his solo until he gets the phrasing just right. And let all of us know that "how" we live our lives—our style—is the most precious gift we can offer our Creator.

Truthless Pietism

Piety is a good word. We usually think of it in a negative way—"She's so pious!" we say in exasperation about a stick-in-the-mud acquaintance. But "piety" can also be a positive description of one's spiritual orientation. To be a "pious" person, in the best sense of the word, is to be a person who practices the essential disciplines of the Christian race.

Piety becomes a bad word only when it is cut off from the truth. As long as piety is hitched to truth, it is a good and necessary quality. Detach it from authentic experience, though, and it becomes that sweet, fake style of religion that the word *pious* often denotes.

When piety is severed from truth, it makes us mouth clichés, sing syrupy songs, and assume the pose of an untroubled angel. Truthless piety is like the house built on the sand: It looks good on the outside but has no foundation beneath it.

Two questions can reveal if we've been seduced by truthless piety. The first is, "Does my piety tell me to deny what I'm feeling?" Some religion tries to sugarcoat life and make it all lovely. Any feelings of doubt, fear, depression, or inadequacy are resolutely denied and denounced as "unspiritual." The Christian, this approach claims, is above such human frailties. When our piety tells us we're not human, that we're exempt from ordinary feelings, it is no longer connected to reality. I'm convinced that God doesn't want us to be superhuman; he wants us to be *fully* human!

The other question that can reveal truthless piety is, "Does my piety make me claim to know more than I really do?" Some people's piety is all-knowing. They know when and how Christ will return, precisely how God inspired Scripture, how many people will be in heaven, and word-by-word what Jesus wrote in the dirt when he knelt before the adulterous woman. In short, their piety removes all of the mystery from life. They have become a religious answering service, ready to give glib answers to any and all seekers. That brand of piety, sadly, is much in evidence today, but it is a far cry from the genuine, searching piety that can enrich our lives.

These four "inside" noises—loveless legalism, graceless activism, artless pragmatism, and truthless pietism—can be heard now in the evangelical world. They all carry a partial truth and therefore sound convincing. But we must turn away from those noises and remember love, grace, style, and honesty. In remembering and living those fundamental qualities, we will be able to run with enthusiasm the race that God has set before us.

Until my first marathon, the longest race I had run was the ten-mile "Shrimp Run" in Galveston, Texas. The race is run every April along the ocean seawall—quite a scenic journey. The race begins just as the sun rises, and daybreak and ocean surf mingle to make every "Shrimp Run" a memorable occasion.

The runners have a choice of distances—two miles, five miles, or ten miles. Last year I felt frisky and entered the longest distance—five miles along the seawall and five miles back. About halfway through the race, I started questioning my choice. Why hadn't I picked the five-miler? Who did I think I was—Frank Shorter? And who in his right mind would want to run ten miles anyway?

Fortunately my family was with me at the race and gave me some positive crowd noise. At the halfway turnaround, they had juice for my parched throat, liniment for my aching knee, a camera to snap my picture, and a ton of kind words for my valiant effort.

On the five-mile return trip, they frequently drove by in the car and shouted needed exhortation. At the finish, all three were clapping, cheering, and nudging me onward. After the race, they had water and glowing words about my "superb form." Honestly, I'm not sure I would have finished that race without them.

Wouldn't it be tremendous if all of us had such encouragement in our spiritual journeys? Wouldn't the race be easier if we had a "cloud of witnesses" rooting for us? Ideally, our church provides a bit of that needed bolstering, and hopefully we can find a few trusted friends who can lift our burdens and share our joys.

But, truthfully, much of the noise we will hear in the race will be distracting and negative. Worldly noise and "religious" noise will be all around us and can lure us from the journey. Our only hope is to recognize these noises for what they are, and then renew our pledge to build a faith that is solid.

In case those distracting crowd noises are the only ones you've been hearing lately, let me be one in the crowd who sounds a different note. "You have a special race to run. God made you unique because without you His world would not be complete. Don't cast your lot with the masses. Stand apart. Run alone if you must, but don't become disillusioned about the race. Listen to the Scriptures. Listen to your heart. And always run to win."

7.
Falling Back

"You were running well; who hindered you from obeying the truth?" (Gal. 5:7).

Competitive runners recognize there is a danger in training too hard for a race. Right beyond the peak performance is staleness. Barely on the other side of maximum effort is burnout.

George Sheehan wrote,

> Just beyond the possibility of doing well as I am able lies the dread condition of overtraining, with its exhaustion and fatigue, its apathy and depression.[1]

Jim Fixx described a condition he called runner's "blahs":

> Sometimes for no clear reason, a runner will feel lackadaisical, uninterested in life around him and depressed. When this happens the cause is almost always overtraining —working too hard and too often for full recovery to occur.[2]

Something similar to runner's "blahs" can happen to us spiritually. Just beyond true commitment is spiritual staleness. Just on the far side of spiritual growth is depression. Sometimes, even in spite of prayer, worship, and Bible study, a lackadaisical attitude creeps in, and the heart waxes cold. Though I have never done a scientific study to prove it, I believe nearly all Christians succumb to this baffling condition at some point in the race.

It happens today, and it happened in the ancient world when the Christian church was being launched. When Paul wrote his letter to the Galatians, those early believers were already losing their fervor. So Paul asked them a pointed question: "You were running well; who hindered you from obeying the truth" (Gal. 5:7)? He went on to describe several problems in the Galatian churches that had caused their "falling back." The Book of Galatians is really a manual for curing the spiritual "blahs," and as such will serve as our resource for dealing with our own apathy.

This condition I'm calling "falling back" can come from a dozen different directions and assume a variety of poses. It can be egged on by a traumatic experience—a divorce, a death, or a betrayal by a Christian friend. It can be prompted by the gnawing fingers of doubt that threaten to squeeze our certitude. It can come upon us as the depression of old age or loneliness. But perhaps the most frustrating of all "falling back" reasons is that nameless apathy which sneaks up on us without any apparent cause. From whatever direction the malady comes, though, most of us are personally acquainted with the "Galatian Syndrome."

Lewis Smedes, a professor at Fuller Theological Seminary, wrote in one of his books about his experience with "falling back." He was staying one autumn in a plain, red cottage at a fishing town in Washington state. He had gone there for three weeks to escape the madness of ordinary life and to consult with his soul. There, in his aloneness, he felt forsaken. He sensed that he could never measure up to others' expectations of him, and that even his family and closest friends could not give him the meaning and acceptance he craved. Clouds of gloom began to overshadow his spirit. Feelings of emptiness crowded into his soul:

> I had never known such lonely pain, never such fear, never such helplessness, never such despair. I was lost, utterly lost. I felt a life of pious trying going down the drain, a life of half-baked belief in grace exposed as futile. I was sunk. I screamed for help, and none could come. I was making my bed in hell.[3]

Whether or not we have ever "bottomed out" to that extent, I have a hunch most of us can identify with his struggle. We know that Paul's question about "falling back" is addressed to us as surely as it was addressed to the Galatians.

Let us turn to our manual for curing the spiritual "blahs"—and see if we can locate needed help for those times when the race is especially difficult. Specifically, let's "zero in" on the verses surrounding Galatians 5:7. Let's detect some of the reasons we "fall back."

Forfeiting Freedom

If I had to pick one word that best captures the theme of Galatians, it would be *freedom.* The entire book is a summons to freedom, a ringing call not to forfeit the liberty Christ purchased at Calvary:

> For freedom Christ has set us free; stand fast therefore, and do not submit again to a yoke of slavery (Gal. 5:1).

> For you were called to freedom, brethren; only do not use your freedom as an opportunity for the flesh, but through love be servants of one another (v. 13).

Paul knew that one sure way of "falling back" in the

race is to forfeit our freedom in Christ.

There are all kinds of bondage that can steal our liberty:

- Bondage to the opinions and expectations of others
- Bondage to harried schedules and pressing commitments
- Bondage to habits that harm us
- Bondage to a past that haunts us
- Bondage to a future that frightens us with its uncertainty
- Bondage to self with its worries, guilt, and feelings of inadequacy
- Bondage to a style of relating to people that discourages closeness

Chains, you see, are a dime a dozen! There is no shortage of factors that wish to enslave us.

But Paul had a specific bondage in mind when he wrote to the Galatians. He was thinking of bondage to the law, a "work-your-way-to-success" style of religion that emphasized circumcision and other works of devotion. The Galatians were being captured by a restrictive religion which elevated legalism and downplayed the freedom of grace.

So, Paul reminded them to shed the chains of the law, to turn their backs on that bondage:

> You are severed from Christ, you who would be justified by the law (v. 14).

> For in Christ Jesus neither circumcision not uncircumcision is of any avail (v. 6).

His anger at those who tried to steal the Galatians' freedom by returning them to the law was obvious: "I wish those who unsettle you would mutilate themselves" (v. 12)!

Paul was consistently the champion of freedom: "For the law of the Spirit of life in Christ Jesus has set me free from the law of sin and death" (Rom. 8:2). He told church after church that forfeiting freedom was a sure way to lag in the race. He knew that "where the Spirit of the Lord is, there is freedom" (2 Cor. 3:17).

In the novel *The Loneliness of the Long Distance Runner*, Smith—the runner in the story—says, "Sometimes I think I've never been as free as during that couple of hours when I'm trotting up the path."[4] Most runners understands what he means. Running is a liberating experience, an opportunity to rid oneself of the shackles of routine and to frolic like a child. To moderns this is one of the most appealing aspects of running. Most of us long to be free from the hectic pace of the day. We are looking for a chance to steal away from the rush and regain our sanity.

Joe Henderson captured this intriguing aspect of running when he wrote,

> Running gives those chances. Every day, you get to run away by yourself. You leave behind the crowd and its orders. You put distance between yourself and the newspapers, magazines, and books that bring you other people's thoughts. You escape the radio and TV, with their packaged voices. You get away from the phone, which can invade your day at any other time.
>
> For an hour a day, you take full command of and responsibility for what you do and think. It is your quietest and calmest and most productive hour. That's when you make friends with yourself and prepare to go back into the crowd on more peaceful terms.[5]

But the follower of Christ senses an even greater freedom. The Christian echoes Smith and testifies, "I've never been as free as when I stand in the shadow of a lonely cross." Ironically, the cross, once a symbol of bondage and execution, has become for us the ultimate picture of freedom. When we look at that cross and come to realize all of its implications, we realize we are free.

Free from what? Free from the popular notion that money determines who we are. Free from a past of sin and guilt. Free from hopelessness. Free from the law which dictates we have to be good enough to please God. Free from the silly trivia that claims so much attention these days. Free from the slavery of trying to please others instead of God.

Because of the cross and its many implications, we are free. Thank God, we are free! And we forfeit that freedom at great cost both to our joy and to our impact on the world.

Cure Number One—Claim and live your freedom.

Giving Up on Grace

Paul's charge against the Galatians was pointed: "You have fallen away from grace" (Gal. 5:4). He was not talking about them losing their salvation, though that verse is often misused to substantiate that improper notion. Paul was talking instead about the graceless activism I mentioned in the last chapter. He was berating the Galatians for trying to run the race without occasional rest stops at the fountain of eternal grace. A foolproof way to stumble into exhaustion is to put our noses to the treadmill of Christian works and forget grace.

It is possible to "fall away from grace" in two different directions: We can fall into legalism or libertinism. Either way, we miss out on the rejuvenation real grace can give us.

If we fall on the side of legalism, we become one of those loveless legalists who keeps the law and lives a life of circumspect misery. Much of Jesus' exhortations to the Pharisees and much of Paul's counsel to the early churches have to do with this bypassing of grace in trying to keep the law. Evidently some in the Galatian churches, too, were so intent on circumcision and "bootstrap" religion that they were guilty of falling away from grace into legalism.

But there were a few, it seems, who fell away from grace into libertinism. Libertinism confuses liberty with license. It misinterprets grace to mean that all restrictions have been removed. While legalism tends to *forget* grace, libertinism tends to *take advantage* of it. Paul wrote to those tending toward libertinism: "Do not use your freedom as an opportunity for the flesh, but through love be servants of one another" (Gal 5:13). And it was to the libertines that Paul listed a whole catalog of "the works of the flesh," and then warned, "Those who do such things shall not inherit the kingdom of God" (v. 21). The Book of Galatians is a reminder that it is possible to miss the joy of grace through the "tightness" of legalism, but that it is also possible to miss it through the "looseness" of libertinism.

So, we who run must forever embrace grace. When we are tired, grace whispers to us, "If God is for us, who is against us" (Rom. 8:31)? When we are ready to quit the race, it shouts, "No, in all these things we are more than conquerors through him that loved us" (v. 37). When we feel unloved and deserted, it reassures us that nothing "will be able to separate us from the love of God in Christ Jesus our Lord" (v. 39). Grace—that incredible, unmerited love gift of God—gives us the boost we need when the hills are steep and the heat unbearable.

Those familiar with the Boston Marathon are acquainted with "Heartbreak Hill." Actually, "Heartbreak Hill" is a series of several hills that dot the course from miles sixteen through twenty-one. Imagine it—when his body is about to "hit the wall," the runner must face a series of grueling hills. Those who run in Boston will tell you this stretch of the Marathon is the "make-it-or-break-it" point.

But runners discover an unexpected boost when, in their struggle up and down the hills, a policeman says through a public-address system, "When you reach the crest of the hill you have six miles to go, and it's all downhill. Your achievement has been superb, and you have my fullest admiration."[6]

That, in effect, is what grace does for those of us who run the Christian race. It reminds us of God's unflagging love, even when our performances are poor. It fills us with the hope that, through his love, we can negotiate any hills life puts in front of us. A clear understanding of God's grace is the best motivator we will ever find for running life's marathon with zest.

Cure Number Two—Know and appreciate God's grace.

Leaving Love

We have already seen that love is the core of Christianity. It comes as no surprise, then, to hear Paul declare that leaving love is another way to get the spiritual "blahs." If we lose the very heart of our calling, how can we ever hope to grasp joy?

Paul cautioned the Galatians about leaving love and making other matters—even virtuous matters—their priority. After telling them that neither circumcision nor uncircumcision earn any points with God, he told them what truly does count—"faith working through love" (Gal. 5:13, author's words). Then he quoted Jesus to underline the importance of loving one another: "For the whole law is fulfilled in one word, 'You shall love your neighbor as yourself' " (Gal. 5:14).

Recall Jesus' words to the Ephesian church in Revelation 2. He lauded their work and their perseverance; he praised them for fending off false teachers; he thanked them for being true to His name. But then He leveled one devastating charge against them: "But I have this against you, that you have abandoned the love you had at first" (Rev. 2:4). Those are sad, sad words. Faithful, persevering, wise—but without love!

When we leave love, we become prime candidates for the spiritual "lows." Some runners will testify to a runner's "high" experience, a time of exhilaration and ecstasy during a long run. But in order to balance the facts, let me testify to experiencing the runner's "low." I have endured some runs that were pure agony. My legs have been heavy, my breathing labored, and my mind too exhausted to spell exhilaration, much less experience it. On those days, I think lion taming is a more sensible avocation than running! When we Christians abandon love and forget it is our primary charter, we will encounter more "lows" than "highs" along the way.

The song went, "Love and marriage go together like a horse and carriage." That may be true, but I have found that love and joy go together like a horse and carriage, too. Love and joy are inseparable. They nourish each other. The more we love, the greater our joy. And the greater our joy, the easier it is to love. Whatever good attributes the Ephesian church had, I can say this about it: It was a joyless church because it had lost its love. And any of us who leave love behind in pursuit of other things can expect a severe case of the spiritual doldrums. Abandoning love always leads to "falling back" in the race.

Cure Number Three—Practice and make your priority a love for people.

Squelching the Spirit

Sometimes we become confused. We think it is normal to be bad, greedy, selfish, and mean. The Christian Way, we think, is hard and unnatural. Eugene Peterson called our thinking into question when he wrote:

> This is as far from the truth as the east is from the west. The easiest thing in the world is to be a Christian. What is hard is to be a sinner. Being a Christian is what we were created for. The life of faith has the support of an entire creation and the resources of a magnificent redemption. The structure of this world was created by God so we could live in it easily and happily as his children. The history we walk in has been repeatedly entered by God, most notably in Jesus Christ, first to show us and then to help us live full of faith and exuberant with purpose. In the course of Christian discipleship we discover that without Christ we were doing it the hard way and that with Christ we are doing it the easy way. It is not Christians who have it hard, but non-Christians.[7]

The Christian life "goes with the flow" of God's design and allows us to fulfill our destiny. For those of us in this race the natural, normal experience is described by Paul in Galatians 5:22-23:

> But the fruit of the Spirit is love, joy, peace, patience, kindness, goodness, faithfulness, gentleness, self-control; against such there is no law.

This is what the Spirit naturally produces within us.

What is unnatural is to squelch the Spirit and prohibit His fruits.

But we can squelch God's natural work within us if we choose. We can give in to our lesser selves, move against the natural flow, yield to temptation, and "fall back" in the race. When we do, we wind up with "the works of the flesh" instead of "the fruits of the Spirit" in our lives:

> fornication, impurity, licentiousness, idolatry, sorcery, enmity, strife, jealousy, anger, selfishness, dissension, party spirit, envy, drunkenness, carousing, and the like (Gal. 5:19-21).

In other words, if we choose we can allow ourselves a painful case of "spiritual indigestion." By eating the wrong foods, we can make our spirits sick. By blunting God's intent for us, we can give ourselves a case of the "blahs." Faith, enthusiasm, and purpose vanish when we dine primarily on junk food.

Understand this: God wants us joyful. He wills meaning, loving relationships, peace, and wonder in our lives. He is *for* us, and the easiest, most natural thing in all the world is to yield to His loving desire.

But we *can* quench His work. We *can* stifle the good things He wants to give us by closing our hearts, by refusing to worship, by forgetting to pray, by disregarding His Word, by withholding our love. Paul wrote to the Thessalonians, "Do not quench the Spirit" (1 Thess. 5:19). That is good advice to anyone who wants to stay spiritually healthy.

Cure Number Four—Listen to and follow the Spirit within you.

These four things—forfeiting freedom, giving up on grace, leaving love, and squelching God's Spirit—can cause us to "fall back." There may be other culprits that would "hinder us from obeying the truth," but these four provide an invaluable checklist for all struggling runners. I hope they help you in your race.

We left Lewis Smedes in anguish. Now let him complete his story:

> I lay down in my spiritual waste. But I did not sink! When I flopped into nothingness I fell into God. The old Hebrew lyricist was right, you can make your bed in hell and find your rest in God's hands. It is not a terrible thing to fall into the hands of the living God. No matter what Jonathan Edwards said. His hands are pierced with nails from Christ's cross; his hands are the strength of his love, the power to hold us and keep us from falling into a hell without God.
>
> I discovered, all by myself, in touch only with my final outpost of feeling, that I could be left, deserted, alone, all my scaffolds knocked down, all the stanchions beneath me pulled away, my buttresses fallen, I could be stripped of human hands, and I could survive. In my deepest heart I survived, stood up, stayed whole, held by nothing at all except the grace of a loving God.[8]

There is the silver lining in what seems to be a very dark spiritual cloud: Even when we "fall back," we fall into the hands of a loving God.

8.
Second Wind

"They who wait for the Lord shall renew their strength,
they shall mount up with wings like eagles,
they shall run and not be weary,
they shall walk and not faint" (Isa. 40:31).

By now your mind may be reeling from all of the ideas I've tossed at you in the preceding chapters. I have already suggested enough "race tips" to keep us busy for a lifetime! If nothing else, the Scriptures we have examined have reminded us that the race is a challenging adventure.

But the very challenge of the pilgrimage can discourage us. How can we ever remember all of this race strategy? And who among us are able to live all of these biblical admonitions? We can actually be overwhelmed by the rigorous demands of the race and grow discouraged about running it.

I'm reminded of the conscientious runner whose well-meaning coach bombarded him with tactics before an upcoming race: "Warm up with these exercises. Keep your stride smooth. Don't go out too fast. Listen for your split times. Don't get trapped in the pack. Make sure Johnson doesn't get too far ahead of you. Run through the tape." By the time his coach finished, the runner was almost too confused to run! The coach could have helped more by simply saying, "Relax. Run easy. We'll be pulling for you."

This is the "relax, run-easy, we'll-be-pulling-for-you" chapter of the book. There are more biblical mandates coming in the remaining chapters, but lest we all become dizzy with advice, we must pause and remember this: Our journey with God is more than the sum of our efforts. Part of the good news of the Bible is that God is involved in our race, too.

One of the most reassuring verses in the whole Bible is Philippians 1:6: "I am sure that he who began a good work in you will bring it to completion at the day of Jesus Christ." That verse is a relaxing reminder that God has a part in our race, too. He launched us on the journey, and He will see us through to the finish line. The race is not only dependent on our competence; its outcome also rests in the hands of God.

Runners speak wistfully of getting their "second wind." There seem to be definite physical changes that bring on this burst of renewed energy:

> It takes about six to ten minutes and a one-degree rise in body temperature to shunt the blood to the working muscles. When that happens, you will experience a light, warm sweat and know what the "second wind" means. You must run quite slowly until this occurs. Then, you can deal yourself to "comfortable," put yourself on automatic pilot and enjoy.[1]

This "second-wind" experience is in no sense a result of the runner's competence. It comes as a rejuvenating gift, a pleasant surprise in the midst of a tough run.

That great verse in the Old Testament, Isaiah 40:31, promises spiritual "second wind" to gasping, exhausted runners:

> They who wait for the Lord shall renew their strength,
> they shall mount up with wings like eagles,
> they shall run and not be weary,
> they shall walk and not faint.

The renewed strength is a gift from God, a life-giving boost unearned and undeserved.

There is tension in the Bible between our works and God's free grace, between our efforts and God's gift of "second wind." The same Paul who tells us to press and strain for the heavenly prize also says, ironically, that our works can never buy God's favor. The same Jesus who commands us to reshape our lives around the truths of the Sermon on the Mount also tells us parables that emphasize the futility of our piety.

There is no easy way to reconcile this tension, but we *can* see it as showing us the meaning of real faith. On the one hand, real faith always proves itself in action. On the other hand, real faith depends solely on the grace of God. Or, to put it in the metaphor of this book, real faith knows it must push for the finish line, but real faith also knows that the race is futile without the "second wind" of God's activity within us.

Most of this book and most of the verses we have examined have dealt with *our* action, *our* initiative, *our* strategy. But simply to make sure we understand both poles in the tension of faith, we look in this chapter at *God's* action, *God's* initiative, and *God's* strategy. We can take heart that God is with us on the journey, quietly moving in the inner recesses of our hearts to bring our lives to completion.

The Prerequisite

Isaiah 40:31 specifies one prerequisite for getting our "second wind." We must "wait on the Lord." The ones who wait will have their strength renewed.

This is not particularly good news to many of us. We are wired for action! None of this waiting-in-silence business! "God," we plead, "give us a program, a checklist of activities, or some spiritual calisthenics that will motivate us. We are ready for 'push and pull' and moving mountains with our muscles. But please, God, don't command silence. Don't order us to be still, to wait upon You, to sit in submission. We can't handle that!"

Runners, generally, are quiet people:

> We distance runners are meditative men. If we have a religious tradition, it is one of non-conformity and withdrawal. . . . At best, we hope for a secluded meadow where we won't be disturbed.[2]

As such, runners go against the grain of our loud, frantic culture.

And those of us who desire the presence of God must periodically flee the noise and chaos of the world, too. We must turn our backs on the activity of modern life and seek a cure for "hurry sickness." We must learn to "wait on the Lord."

It will not be easy. It will mean turning off the television, or taking a trip without the radio screaming at us. It will mean getting up early to think and pray, or taking a stroll around the block at sunset. It will mean retreating to a cottage somewhere like Lewis Smedes did, or strapping on some running shoes and taking a long jaunt on a secluded road. Learning to be still and wait will not be easy in a society that worships activity.

But it *is* the prerequisite to "second wind." We will never have quiet intimacy with God if we are always in a hurry. Calvin Miller reminded us:

> Intimacy may not be rushed. To meet with the Son of God takes time. We have learned all too well the witless art of living fast. We gulp our meals sandwiched between pressing obligations. The table of communion with Christ is not a fast-food franchise. We cannot dash into his presence and

choke down inwardness before we hurry to our one o'clock appointment. Inwardness is time-consuming, open only to minds willing to sample spirituality in small bites, savoring each one. It is difficult to teach the unhurried discipline of the table to a culture so used to frozen dinners and condensed novels.[3]

Pascal, the brilliant Frenchman, once wrote, "I have often said that all the troubles of man come from him not knowing how to sit still."[4] There is no doubt that many of the troubles that come to us can be traced to our unwillingness to sit still and commune with God. Many of us are busy *for* the Lord, but never slow down to let Him get busy *in* us!

The biblical material inviting us to slow down and meet God is plentiful. Here's a small sampling:

Be still, and know that I am God (Ps. 46:10).

Commune with your own hearts upon your beds, and be silent (Ps. 4:4).

Thou dost keep him in perfect peace,
whose mind is stayed on thee,
because he trusts in thee (Isa. 26:3).

In returning and rest you shall be saved;
in quietness and in trust shall be your strength (Isa. 30:15).

Come to me, all who labor and are heavy laden, and I will give you rest (Matt. 11:28).

Peace I leave with you; my peace I give to you; not as the world gives do I give to you. Let not your hearts be troubled, neither let them be afraid (John 14:27).

Have no anxiety about anything, but in everything by

prayer and supplication with thanksgiving let your re-
quests be made known to God. And the peace of God,
which passes all understanding, will keep your hearts and
minds in Christ Jesus (Phil 4:6-7).

So then, there remains a sabbath rest for the people of
God; for whoever enters God's rest also ceases from his
labors as God did from his (Heb. 4:9-10).

All the way through the Bible we are beckoned to flee
those trivial pursuits marked by noisy activity to meet our
God in the stillness.

But this waiting to which the prophet calls us in Isaiah
40:31 is not merely the absence of noise. We are to wait
for the Lord. The prophet was not advocating passive
resignation; he was calling for positive expectation. In the
silence away from the chattering crowd, we are to expect
God to reveal Himself. We are to trust and keep on trusting that God will honor our solitude.

This verse was originally addressed to people in exile,
in a strange land desperately needing a ray of hope. The
prophet's word was, "Hope in God. Expect Him to sus-
tain. Keep on keeping on even in the darkness of the
moment."

There is something in the verse that reminds me of
Jesus' advice on prayer: "Keep on asking, and it will be
given you; keep on seeking, and you will find; keep on
knocking, and it will be opened to you" (Matt. 7:7, author's translation). Both Isaiah 40:31 and Matthew 7:7 are
talking about persistent faith, a faith for the long run.

Of course, we would wish it otherwise. We would like
quick solutions, "presto" programs, and three easy steps
to abundant living. Patience comes hard for all of us. But
"waiting for the Lord" implies that "long obedience" I referred to earlier. In a quiet, consistent relationship with

God we steady our souls on something sturdier that a "passing fancy."

All of the worthwhile things in life take time. We can't cultivate character overnight. We can't reach fulfillment in a seminar. We can't garner spiritual depth in one sermon. We can't give our children faith in an annual Easter visit to church. All of those come only "in the long run," only as we "wait for the Lord."

I think this is one of the often overlooked truths Jesus revealed about happiness in the Beatitudes. The Beatitudes state, without question, that there are no shortcuts to happiness. We will find "blessedness" of life only as we acquire those other qualities Jesus mentioned—poverty of spirit, mourning, meekness, hungering and thirsting after righteousness, mercy, purity of heart, peacemaking, and being persecuted for righteousness' sake. Those people wanting instant happiness will not like Jesus' Beatitudes. He makes happiness a by-product of life qualities that come only in "waiting for the Lord."

A part of our strategy for running the race, then, must include this willingness to wait, to relax and let God work in us, and to rest our lives patiently in His care. As strange as it sounds, sometimes the only way to move ahead in the race is to stand still!

Busy schedules, pushy people, and jangling noises will continue to clamor for our attention. But we cannot yield to them, not if we want "second wind":

> Sometimes it is all fruitless. I lack the patience, the submission, the letting go. There are, after all, things to be done. People waiting. Projects uncompleted. Letters to be answered. Paperwork to do. Planes to be caught. A man can waste just so much time and no more waiting for inspiration.

But I must wait. Wait and listen. That inner stillness is the only way to reach these inner marvels all of us possess.[5]

The Promise

"Those who wait for the Lord shall renew their strength"—that is the promise. The waiting will prompt the "second wind." The time invested in stilling our hearts will reap dividends of new strength. God will respond and reward our search.

But His response cannot be programmed. Isaiah 40:31 suggests three different ways God may give us new strength. In his book, *Tracks of a Fellow Struggler,* John Claypool identified these three forms of help as ecstasy, strength for activism, and perseverance. To make them easier to remember, let's call them ecstasy, energy, and endurance. The "second wind" may come in any of these three forms.

Ecstasy

At times, God's response enables us to "mount up with wings like eagles." He dissolves a tumor, removes an obstacle, transforms a hard heart, or in some other miraculous way lifts us above a problem. We soar with the eagles, for God is close and life is precious.

Some years ago, Richard Bach was diligently seeking a publisher for a story he had written. But all of the publishers he approached questioned its marketability. They didn't know how to classify the book. Was it a children's story? An adult story? A novel? A self-help book? It didn't seem to fit comfortably in any of those categories.

Finally, one company gambled and published the book. *Jonathan Livingston Seagull* became a huge best-seller and was later made into a movie. The tale of Jonathan wanting to soar above the mediocrity of other gulls must have hit a responsive chord in millions of people. I guess it is because Jonathan's quest to shun the humdrum and fly with the eagles is our quest, too. We want life to be throbbing with meaning.

And there are times when God gives us that ecstasy. He enables us "to mount up with wings like eagles," to live with a lump in our throats and tears of joy in our eyes.

One way God gives us "second wind" in the race is to intervene with miracle and wonder. When He reveals Himself in such ecstasy we can only be humbly grateful and then glory in the awesome experience of flying with eagles.

Energy

But God doesn't always give the gift of ecstasy. Sometimes He presents the gift of energy. Because we have "waited for the Lord," we can "run and not be weary." We are not given wings and lifted *out* of a situation, but we are given the energy to move victoriously *through* it. God's response takes the form of infused vitality and creativity. We sense His presence with us and find unusual strength for living through a dilemma.

Every runner would like to have just one race where he could "run and not be weary." I marveled at the pace of gold-medalist Carlos Lopes in the 1984 Olympic marathon. Somewhere late in the race—around the twenty-mile mark—the thirty-seven-year-old banker from Portugal ran a 4:41 mile. After nineteen or twenty tough miles, he had the energy to run a 4:41 mile! That is almost miraculous! But it provides a picture for us of one who, after long miles in the race, still had the energy to "run and not be weary."

This divine energy we receive in life usually comes disguised as ordinary events and normal people. Someone calls us long-distance. We happen upon just the book we need. A friend takes us to lunch. Someone affirms our work. The preacher's sermon is especially timely. We discover a new hobby or interest. Those common, unspectacular things make all the difference in our energy level. Without them, we limp sullenly down the track. With them, we can "run and not be weary." And somewhere behind them all is One who works in silence and mystery to bring our lives to completion.

Endurance

The third kind of help God sometimes chooses to bestow is endurance: "they shall walk and not faint." Given a choice we would always take the ecstasy of flying with eagles or the energy of running and not being weary. But the third gift, endurance, is not to be taken lightly. It, too, is a valuable gift to those who "wait for the Lord." The strength just to take another step or just to get through another day is wonderful help in some dark situations.

The old man is dying. He has known both heartache and heroism in his lifetime. He has been the leader of a great people and has taken them to the doorstep of a new adventure. But he is too old to make the journey. He has passed the leadership to a younger man. And now he stands to offer his final blessing to his beloved people. He addresses tribe after tribe, giving counsel and promise to each. When he comes to the tribe of Asher, Moses says, "As your days, so shall your strength be" (Deut. 33:25).

What a blessing! What a great promise to cling to in the night! Strength enough for each day. Sustenance for every step along the journey. The tribe of Asher knew after Moses' blessing that it could "walk and not faint."

Dr. Claypool says this gift of endurance was the gift given to him when his young daughter suffered from and

finally died of leukemia. In the midst of that awful darkness, he could say:

> I confess to you honestly that I have no wings with which
> to fly or even any legs on which to run—but listen, by the
> grace of God, I am still on my feet! I have not fainted yet.
> I have not exploded in the anger of presumption, nor have
> I keeled over into the paralysis of despair. All I am doing
> is walking and not fainting, hanging in there, enduring
> with patience what I cannot change but have to bear.
>
> This may not sound like much to you, but to me it is the
> most appropriate gift of all. My religion has been the diff-
> erence in the last two weeks; it has given me the gift of
> patience, the gift of endurance, the strength to walk and
> not faint. And I am here to give thanks to God for that![6]

We cannot predict how God will reveal himself to us
when we wait upon him. Sometimes, no doubt, we will
get the ecstasy of miracles. At other times, we will receive
the energy to run boldly and not be weary. And sometimes we will get strength for the day, the gift to just
"hang in there" and endure.

But our hope—and the promise of Isaiah 40:31—is that
God is never deaf to our pleas. Asking, seeking, knocking,
and waiting *do* get results. God will honor our expectant
waiting with His presence.

It disturbs me that so many of us "good Christians" are
busy, irritable, uptight, and frustrated. The writer of the
Book of Hebrews says those who know Christ have entered into His rest. Somehow we modern Christians have
entered into His frenzy! We are straining, struggling runners and poor advertisements for the abundant life.

We urgently need "second wind," and we will not get
it until we slow down and "wait for the Lord." Renewed

strength—in whatever form God gives it—will come only to those who meet the prerequisite of waiting.

Tim Hansel began his book *When I Relax, I Feel Guilty* with a prayer written by Orin L. Crain. The prayer calls all of us "busy Christians" to reconsider our ways:

Slow me down, Lord.

Ease the pounding of my heart by the quieting of my mind.

Steady my hurried pace with a vision of the eternal reach of time.

Give me, amid the confusion of the day, the calmness of the everlasting hills.

Break the tensions of my nerves and muscles with the the soothing music of the singing streams that live in my memory.

Teach me the art of taking minute vacations—of slowing down to look at a flower, to chat with a friend, to pat a dog, to smile at a child, to read a few lines from a good book.

Slow me down, Lord, and inspire me to send my roots deep into the soil of life's enduring values, that I may grow toward my greater destiny.

Remind me each day that the race is not always to the swift; that there is more to life than increasing its speed.

Let me look upward to the towering oak and know that it grew great and strong because it grew slowly and well.[7]

When we can pray like that, we will learn the meaning of "second wind."

9.
Picking Up the Pace

"Therefore, since we are surrounded by so great a cloud of witnesses, let us also lay aside every weight, and sin which clings so closely, and let us run with perseverance the race that is set before us, looking to Jesus the pioneer and perfecter of our faith" (Heb. 12:1-2).

In running jargon, "L.S.D." is not a drug. "L.S.D." means "long, slow distance," a style of training popularized by Joe Henderson in a book by that name in 1969. In "L.S.D." training, a runner runs long distances at a slow, comfortable pace. The emphasis is on relaxed, enjoyable running, not speed.

Most "fun runners" like myself use the "L.S.D." method, even if they've never heard the term. We recreational runners are not usually after records or trophies. We want to jog along in comfort, smell the flowers and freshly-mowed grass, and stay reasonably fit. We want running to be fun, not a strenuous ordeal.

Give me a choice between running six miles at a slow pace or three miles at a fast one, and I will pick the six-mile jaunt every time. I can find a pace that is easy for me and run for miles without exhaustion. But ask me to pick up the pace and my body immediately rebels. It complains if it is pushed too hard. As I have trained for some of the local races, it has angrily threatened to quit if I didn't pamper it some.

Stretching or pushing our spirits usually yields a similar response. Picking up the pace spiritually is hard to do. Most of us have settled into a comfortable pace, one we have maintained for years. We go to church, give a certain percent of our money to Christian causes, do our jobs, love our families, pray periodically, and generally feel good about life.

But somewhere deep within us is a little voice that whispers, "You need to be challenged. You're not stretching your soul. You're stagnating spiritually. You need to pick up the pace."

When we hear that voice, we must give it careful attention. That voice could be God's Spirit trying to break through our casual routine to prod us to change. It could be a life-renewing call to flee contentment and complacency to find the abundant life.

The Christian life is not for settlers; it is for pioneers. When we settle into a cozy rut, we become prime candidates for the "Laodicean Syndrome"—that spiritual lethargy that makes our Christianity lukewarm.

The call to follow Jesus was to the early disciples—and should be today—a call to pioneer, to test new waters, to probe for adventure. One of the most stinging indictments against the modern church is the one that accuses it of being boring. Followers of Jesus boring? Worship humdrum? Discipleship a drag? No! Not unless we turn the race into a quilting party for settlers! If the race is a life-and-death contest for pioneers, it can never be boring.

So how can we pick up the pace? What can we do to challenge and push ourselves to change? That great running passage in the Book of Hebrews offers us four clues. Hopefully there is something in Hebrews 12:1-2 that can motivate us to run better. I have condensed the truths of these two verses to four key verbs: remember, simplify, persevere, and concentrate.

Remember

Occasionally our family gets out the picture albums and spends some time reminiscing. Flipping through the albums always engenders some interesting comments:

> You were a little hefty back then, weren't you? I think the Cowboys could've used you at defensive tackle!

> Who's the hippie here? I don't ever remember your hair being that long!

> Can you believe the dresses were so short back then? My goodness, that's nearly indecent!

> Look at how these kids have grown! It seems just yesterday that we took these baby pictures.

> Oh my goodness, I look atrocious in that picture! Here, let me take that one and burn it!

Why do we do all of that? Why do we buy cameras, snap pictures, paste them in albums, and spend evenings poking fun at each other? I think we do those things for one reason—we want to remember who we are.

When we browse through those snapshots we're remembering our identity—this is where we used to live; this is how we celebrate Christmas; this is what we looked like. The journey through the photo album is really a journey into ourselves and our past. Each photo touches a memory cell somewhere in our brain, and we are able to remember.

Remembering is important. It gives us a heritage and a sense of identity. It enables us to know who we are and *whose* we are. Without memory, we would all be impoverished. We would be like cut flowers with no understanding of the roots that have nourished us.

The writer of the Book of Hebrews, in calling those
early Christians to pick up the pace, wrote, "Therefore
since we are surrounded by so great a cloud of witnesses."
He had just called the roll of faith in Hebrews 11. One
after another he had mentioned Old Testament heroes
and heroines who had been pacesetters in the race. Then
he called his readers to remember those pacesetters and
to picture those heroes and heroines in the grandstands
cheering them on. The first clue he offered them was a
reminder to remember, to use memory as a motivator.

We modern Christians must also stir up the gift of memory. The race we are running is really a relay that has been
going on for centuries. Those the writer of Hebrews mentioned ran valiantly and passed the baton to their children
and grandchildren. They, in turn, lived the faith, wrote
songs and poems, worshiped in their own way, ministered
as they could, and passed the baton to the next generation. And the relay has continued to this day. You and I
have received the baton from our parents and grandparents, and now we run. And we hope that when our race
is finished, our children, or others we have loved, will take
the baton and go with it.

This "relay race" perspective helps us realize that
Christianity is no Johnny-come-lately fad. God has been
touching and calling people for thousands of years. Discipleship is not a hula-hoop craze. Faith is not a fly-by-night
whim. For centuries and centuries, God has been inviting
people to run the race and build a Kingdom. You and I are
but the latest in a long line who have said "yes" to the call.

This heritage we have will motivate us if we know about
it. Read of Moses, David, and Jeremiah in the Old Testament and see if their journey doesn't grip you. Read of
Jesus, Peter, Paul, and John in the New Testament and see
if you're not inspired. Snoop through the history books,

learn about the Christian martyrs, and see if you're not moved by their commitment. Learn of the sufferings of the Anabaptists and see if you don't feel better about being a member of a Baptist church. Or just flip through the photo albums as our family does and see if mother, father, grandpa, grandma, and Aunt Kate don't bring to memory both fun and faith.

If we are "cut-flower" Christians without any sense of heritage, we will find the race difficult. If we don't know our history, if we have no heroes and heroines of faith to stir us, we will find it hard to stay in the race. But if we are surrounded by a great cloud of witnesses, we will have a continual source of motivation and inspiration.

If you want to pick up the pace, remember those who have run before you got the baton.

Simplify

Early in this book we anticipated the hurdle of clutter. Hebrews 12:1 calls us to look again at streamlining life: "let us also lay aside every weight, and sin which clings so closely." We are to shed excess baggage and crystallize life down to what is ultimately important.

Picture, if you can, a marathoner on the starting line encumbered with an overcoat and holding a piece of luggage in each hand. The thought is ludicrous because marathoners always streamline their apparel. Lightweight shorts, a flimsy T-shirt, and running shoes would be about all any runner would ever wear. In marathoning, the rule in clothing is the less the better. Some runners even get a haircut before a big race to reduce wind resistance!

Part of the joy of running is its simplicity. Running is a simple sport devoid of gadgets, complex rules, and complicated equipment. Give a person some decent running

shoes and he or she can take it from there. Running and
runners are marked by simplicity:

> For the runner, less is better. The life that is his work of
> art is understated. His friends and wants are few, he can
> be captured in a few strokes. One friend, a few clothes, a
> meal now and then, some change in his pockets; and, for
> enjoyment, his thoughts and the elements.[1]

But too many of us trying to run "God's marathon" are
burdened with the topcoat and baggage. We who follow
the one who taught and lived the simple life have become
as encumbered as the next guy. Our lives seem to be as
hurried and scattered as the ones who don't know Christ.
It is time to "lay aside those weights and the sin which
clings so closely" and simplify our existence.

Can we do it? Is the simple life even possible in our
technological age? Yes, it is possible—but not easy or
"natural." To do it, we need to understand the individual
areas of our lives that need changing. Simplicity of life can
come only as we recognize the specific "weights" that we
must "lay aside."

First, we can simplify our possessions. As Americans
caught up in the madness of consumerism, we have a
passion to possess. We even measure our worth by how
many expensive trinkets we can acquire. G.K Chesterton
once said, "There are two ways to get enough; one is to
continue to accumulate more and more. The other is to
desire less."[2] We Americans nearly always choose the first
option.

Some of those in that heavenly cloud of witnesses that
now surrounds us could teach us a thing or two about
simplicity of possessions. Hudson Taylor, the missionary to
China, once wrote:

> I soon found that I could live upon very much less than I had previously thought possible. Butter, milk, and other luxuries I ceased to use, and found that by living mainly on oatmeal and rice, with occasional variations, a very small amount was sufficient for my needs. . . . My experience was that the less I spent on myself and the more I gave to others, the fuller of happiness and blessing did my soul become.[3]

John Wesley, the founder of Methodism, once purportedly told his sister, "Money never stays with me. It would burn me if it did. I throw it out of my hands as soon as possible, lest it should find its way within my heart."[4] He told everyone that if at his death he had more than ten pounds in his possession (about $23) people could call him a robber.

The stark simplicity and voluntary poverty of Taylor and Wesley stand in sharp contrast to our sumptuous lifestyles. But their vibrant lives make us pause long enough to wonder who really experiences life—the ones who simplify life to serve God or the ones who complicate life to serve self? Think about it—if you dare.

Second, we can simplify our activities. We picture the "successful" person in our culture as the one who is always "on the go," attending meetings, flitting from activity to activity. We Christians have fallen for that mirage without bothering to examine it very closely. Actually, the man "on the go" is not successful; he's tired and superficial. The woman who jumps from business conference to civic club to PTA is not brimming with life; she's worn to a frazzle.

A decision to try the simple life obligates us to condense our schedule to those activities that really have meaning. We don't have to be at every meeting or shake every hand or ramrod every school carnival. We can choose those activities that suit our schedule and our activities, but then leave time to rest, work jigsaw puzzles with the kids, and sip cocoa on the back porch.

To fall prey to the "busy means successful" trap is a sure way to wear ourselves down to a frenzied nub. It will also ensure that we will never pick up the pace in the race God has set before us.

Third, we can simplify our speech. How much of what we say has any value? It is now thought quite normal to babble on about anything just to drown the awful sound of silence. It is quite acceptable now to stretch the truth or tell "white lies" to cover our mistakes.

But the simple life also includes simplicity of speech. If we are to follow Jesus, our yes must be yes and our no must be no. Unless we can improve on silence, we must hold our tongues. Those who live simply usually listen much more than they talk.

Fourth, we can simplify our thoughts. This, I think, is the real key to simplicity. We must not be naive, ignorant, or uninformed, but we must be simpleminded! The simple life always flows from a simple, uncluttered mind.

I am often overwhelmed by the details that clutter my brain—change the oil in the car, call John, fix the lock on the back door, visit Mrs. Jones in the hospital, cash a check at the bank, have a "quiet time," help the kids with homework, write a piece for the church newsletter. And that's just Monday's clutter! Tuesday's is even worse!

But that clutter must not bog me down so that I lose my way in life. Sometimes I have to sweep that clutter away and remind myself that I am not here to run errands and chase rabbits. I am here to build a Kingdom!

In *Freedom of Simplicity*, Richard Foster wrote,

In the final analysis we are not the ones who have to

untangle all the intricacies of our complex world. There are not many things we have to keep in mind—in fact, only one: to be attentive to the voice of the true Shepherd. There are not many decisions we have to make—in fact, only one: to seek first his Kingdom and his righteousness. There are not many tasks we have to do—in fact, only one: to obey him in all things.[5]

I find it interesting that the Desert Fathers, who renounced all worldly things to concentrate on God, called themselve *Athletae Dei,* the athletes of God. They knew they had to strip away all hindrances if they were to run well in the race.

And we must know that, too. Simplicity is a must if we want to pick up the pace.

Persevere

Do you remember Rosie Ruiz? She astounded the running world some years ago when she was the first female finisher at the Boston Marathon. Her previous race times had been mediocre, and no one expected her to be among the leaders. And she looked so fresh at the finish line!

An investigation later revealed that Rosie had "fudged" a bit. She hadn't actually run the entire 26.2-mile course and was promptly disqualified. The rules at Boston are the same as the rules at any respectable race—the participants must start at the proper place, run the specified course, and cross the finish line. It would certainly not be fair to award the trophy to one who just "waltzed in" the final few miles of the course. The winner must be one who persevered, conquered all the obstacles, and crossed the line first.

Perseverance has been a continuing theme of this book. Hebrews 12:1 reminds us again of the necessity of "a long obedience": "let us run with perseverance the race that is set before us." We have seen over and over that the race is a marathon, not a dash. Scripture after Scripture has challenged us to plan for a long run and to endure to the end. Those who try to run the Christian race like Rosie ran Boston will be disqualified by the Judge at the finish line.

To try to pull together the truths about persevering we have learned so far—and perhaps to add a few new ones—I offer you "Ten Tips for Weary Runners." When you are winded and your spirit is as dry as dust, I hope some of these tips can help you "hang in there."

Ten Tips for Weary Runners

1. *Don't confuse faith and feelings.* Feelings are fickle. Some days we will not feel particularly "Christian." The finest saint among us will occasionally feel lifeless, grumpy, or depressed. But faith rests on a covenant, not an emotional roller coaster.

2. *Affirm your beliefs, not your doubts.* On our darkest days, when God seems most distant, we still have some theological linchpins that can hold our faith together. We can think of Christ, the cross, the resurrection, and other foundational truths. Affirming what we *do* believe will keep us from being swallowed by doubt.

3. *Don't let others determine your course.* Others cannot run the race for us. Each of us has a special journey, a unique personality, a one-of-a-kind relationship to God. When we deny our individuality and forfeit our uniqueness, we squelch what God wants to do in and through us. Many a weary runner would get an injection of energy by taking "the road less traveled."

4. *Get in shape physically and emotionally.* The pieces of the personhood puzzle always interconnect. We cannot separate the spiritual dimension of our lives from the physical and emotional dimensions. If one of those areas

suffers, the others usually do, too. If one improves, the others improve as well. When we get spiritually tired, we can often pick up the pace by getting in better shape physically and emotionally.

5. *Call a "time out" to reconsider your strategy.* Weariness and unrest can actually be blessings if they stimulate us to change. If we continually find ourselves spiritually depleted, our heart is trying to tell us something. Just as fever signals physical infection, so misery warns us of a spiritual disease. At times, we have to heed those warnings, inventory our lives, and do some serious overhauling.

6. *Let God carry His rightful load.* Playing God will always sap us, but still we try. When Jesus asks, "Which of you by being anxious can add one cubit to his span of life?" (Matt. 6:27), we answer an eager, "I can!" But the point of the question is that God has assumed responsibility for His world. He provides for the birds of the air and dresses the lilies of the field in royal gowns. And He offers to give us rest from our burdens. It's OK for us to be human, to relax, and to let God be God.

7. *Lean on others when you're exhausted.* A few good friends can make the race bearable when the going gets hard. All of us need someone we can be honest with, someone with whom we can be truly ourselves. Paul's advice to "Bear one another's burdens" (Gal. 6:2) is always good race strategy.

8. *Remember that both summer and winter are needed seasons of the soul.* No one wants weariness or discouragement. But there are lessons to be learned in those "down times" than we can learn at no other time. Faith is forged in the cold darkness of the soul's winter.

9. *Don't let the present or the past dictate your future.* Today's confusion doesn't necessarily mean that we are

permanently stuck in that condition. And yesterday's worries don't have to cast a shadow on tomorrow's opportunities. God said, "Behold I make all things new" (Rev. 21:5), so we can live with hope. With Robert Browning we can trust that "the best is yet to be."

10. *Seek God even when He is silent.* The true test of our faith is how we do when God is silent. Anyone can run with enthusiasm when God is near and life is rosy. But to run with patience when we feel helpless, to preach, pray, and seek God when our spirits are downcast is the real measure of our commitment.

Those ten tips come out of my own experience. I have had some "dark nights of the soul," times when God seemed a fairy tale. But in heeding some of these suggestions myself, I have never despaired. Through it all I've learned that I *can* endure and that the sun will eventually shine again.

Concentrate

The fourth clue tucked away in Hebrews 12:1-2 is concentration. The writer bade us to pick up the pace by "looking to Jesus the pioneer and perfecter of our faith." We are to focus our gaze on the One who pioneered and perfected the race. In looking at Him we will gain renewed vigor for the race we must run.

I still remember the shock I received when I got my first pair of glasses. Gradually, imperceptibly my vision had deteriorated, and I was hardly aware of it. But when I put on those glasses at the optometrist's office, I gasped at the things I saw! I peered out the office window and saw distinct letters on a sign across the street. I saw individual leaves on trees and specific facial features in a crowd of people. I didn't know it was possible to see so clearly!

When we "look to Jesus" a similar thing happens to our spiritual eyesight. We begin to see life through new eyes.

Christ becomes the lens through which we see everything, and, as Paul put it, "the old has passed away, behold, the new has come" (2 Cor. 5:17).

When we look at our possessions through the lens of Christ, for example, we see them not as status symbols or merit badges, but as tools to use in loving others. Those who are not "looking to Jesus" will never understand our perspective because they're not wearing our "glasses." But those of us who know Him will always see our worth as completely detached from our possessions.

When we look at personal relationships with our new eyes, we will know that we cannot just cater to those who enhance our career or promote our reputation. We will have to love—period. Love the unlovely. Love the hungry, the poor, the sick, the "least of these."

When we look at happiness, we will understand that it is more than garnering pleasure, power, and possessions. We will begin to see that happiness is loving God and living with the servant's heart.

When we gaze at salvation, we will see that it doesn't involve piling up achievement awards to impress God or struggling to the top of the morality ladder. We will know that salvation hinges on the cross, and then gladly abandon ourselves to grace.

When we experience suffering, we will perceive that our pain is not meaningless and that God is not playing cruel tricks on us. We will pray that our suffering will somehow be redemptive, that some good will come from that bad situation.

And when we look at death with our new eyes, we will no longer see it as the ultimate disaster. We will mourn when a loved one dies, but we will not grieve as those who have no hope. Because Jesus said, "I go to prepare a place for you" (John 14:2), we will see even death as a doorway.

Do you see the difference Jesus makes? When we concentrate on Him, and look at life *through* Him, all things become new. We get transformed vision and new energy for the race. Concentrating on Him always motivates us to pick up the pace.

A friend dropped by my office recently to gloat about a race he had run. His time hadn't been particularly impressive, but he was thrilled, anyway. The reason? The fastest of his six miles had been the last. After five long miles, he had been able to pick up the pace and come home in style. I excused his pride because I thought he had reason to brag. Picking up the pace in a grueling 10-K *is* an achievement.

But that achievement pales beside the accomplishments of those people who pick up the pace spiritually. I stand in awe of the husband and wife who, in mid-life, decide to serve as foreign mission volunteers. I applaud the woman who, after raising her children, enrolls at seminary to sharpen her theological perception. I congratulate that man who leaves the security of the corporate world to try his hand at preaching the Good News in a country church. I marvel at the commitment of the millionaire who drops out of the rat race to build homes for poor people. Those folks are in the lineage of the heroes and heroines of Hebrews 11.

Really, I suppose it is almost miraculous when any of us chooses to risk and pick up the pace. Ruts are comfortable. We all grow cozy in them. But for Christian people, ruts are for leaving. We are, by calling, pioneers. We follow one who was "the pioneer and perfecter of our faith." So any time a rut appears, we forsake it. And any time the race gets too easy, we suspect it's time to pick up the pace.

10.
Gun Lap

"Not that I have already obtained this or am already per-fect; but I press on to make it my own, because Christ Jesus has made me his own. Brethren, I do not consider that I have made it my own; but one thing I do, forgetting what lies behind and straining forward to what lies ahead, I press on toward the goal for the prize of the upward call of God in Christ Jesus" (Phil. 3:12-14).

I saw a book on running the other day that made me chuckle. On the cover were a man and woman—presumably husband and wife—running together. They were dressed in natty sportswear and had contented smiles on their faces. They looked like lovers on an afternoon romp.

I chuckled because I thought of the runs my wife and I often take together. We would never make the jacket of a book! Our running attire is old and faded, and we seldom smile when we run. (I can't get Sherry to talk, much less smile!) By journey's end, our faces are flushed, our hair tousled, our wind exhausted, and our clothes soaked with sweat. A photographer at the finish line would find us poor advertisements for the joy of running.

I have a friend who is convinced that runners have a serious emotional problem. "They're psychologically sick," he asserts. "They have this unconscious need to punish themselves." At the end of some of those strenuous, sweat-soaked runs, I get the feeling he might be right.

But our exhaustion would be a more accurate portrayal of running than the picture of the couple "tiptoeing through the tulips." Our pain and perspiration *are* parts of the running experience. If you want to dress fancy and pose for book covers, you'd best try another sport. For all of its rewards, running does involve *work*.

Life does, too. Sometimes life is grim business, and we are forced to strain and sweat just to survive. Those people who tell us that life can be continuously wonderful if we'll just try their program or their product are not being completely candid with us. Even those Christians who promise us constant ecstasy are being less than honest. In truth, Christians also know the pain and perspiration of life.

When Paul wrote the Book of Philippians, life had backed him into a corner—literally! He was in prison— probably in Rome—and facing persecution. He was not a young man and had already been knocked around by life. I suppose we could call this part of Paul's life "the gun lap phase." It was late in the race, the pressure was on, and it was time to press on to the finish line. He was living with stress, uncertainty, and with having to cope with less-than-ideal circumstances.

All of us have been—or will be—in this "gun lap phase" of the race. We will have to deal with pressure and trouble and then try to do our best under adverse running conditions. Because Paul had already run the race and faced the tension of the gun lap, his words to the Philippians can help us run better when we are tense or troubled. In this chapter, we will focus on three verses in Philippians 4 that give us in capsule form Paul's strategy for running the gun lap.

The surprising thing, considering the circumstances, is the upbeat tone of Philippians. In spite of his situation, Paul wrote of "joy" six times in the letter and used the word *rejoice* twelve times. Philippians is perhaps the most optimistic of all of Paul's biblical correspondence, even though it was written in the tense "gun lap period" of his life. The buoyant ring of the book gives us great hope that Paul can share with us the secret of running the gun lap.

When we look at Philippians 3:12-14, we see that Paul was telling us to remember some specific ideas. In the last chapter, "Picking Up the Pace," we saw the importance of remembering our heritage, of knowing of that "so great a cloud of witnesses" that has run before us. In this passage, Paul called to our attention other truths that can uplift us when stress threatens to kill our joy. When a "gun lap situation" faces us, it is time, Paul said, to remember.

Remember the Firm Grip of Christ

For one thing, we can remember the firm grip Christ has on our lives. Not only do we have a commitment *to Him;* he also has a commitment *to us.* Paul expressed it this way, "I press on to make it my own, because Christ Jesus has made me his own." William Barclay translates Paul's words, "I press on to try to grasp that for which I have been grasped by Jesus Christ."

We are in the sure grasp of Christ! Even when we feel we don't have Him, He has us. Even when circumstance steals our assurance, He doesn't forsake us. We are held secure in His loving hands.

That truth will steady the shakiest runner! Because we know He holds us and that He is working in us, we do not give up when we must face the pressure of a "gun lap situation." With the writer of the Book of Hebrews we can say, "Let us hold fast the confession of our hope without wavering, for he who promised is faithful" (Heb. 10:23). If Christ has us in His hands, who or what can harm us?

I think being in the grip of Christ meant at least two things to Paul: It meant Christ had gripped him with *mercy,* and it meant Christ had gripped him for *ministry.*

In 2 Corinthians 4:1, Paul alluded to both of these things when he wrote, "Therefore, having this ministry by the mercy of God, we do not lose heart." Paul did not lose heart because he had mercy and a ministry.

Tragically, many today *are* "losing heart." All of those dreary statistics on drug and alcohol abuse, suicide, and severe depression are stark reminders that people all around us are "losing heart." And we hope and pray that it will never happen to us. We want to stay alive—truly alive—all of our days. We want to be able to say with Paul that, though our outer self is decaying, our inner self is being renewed every day.

The way to keep our inner self renewed is to follow Paul's two-pronged counsel—to receive mercy and to practice ministry.

To receive mercy means we live by grace. We know that our lives rest in the love of God, a love that stumbled to Calvary and died there to prove itself. Paul knew he was a sinner, and, in fact, labeled himself "the foremost of sinners" (1 Tim. 1:15). He had persecuted the church, consented to the stoning of Stephen, and generally lived a life of egocentric morality. Then God touched him on the Damascus road, and he learned about mercy. He became the great apostle of grace, boldly telling others of the miraculous mercy of God. Even in prison, his spirits were lifted when he thought about God's unwarranted care: "I can do all things in him who strengthens me" (Phil. 4:13).

To have a ministry is to have a purpose. When Christ grips us, He grips us to serve a specific role. For Paul, that role was preaching, establishing churches, and launching the Christian movement. But ministry doesn't have to be a task formally ordained by a church. Ministry is any special purpose we have—loving a spouse, taking delight in a child, teaching a class, befriending a stranger, building a house with care. Those "ministries" give us a passion for living. Without them, we are destined to "lose heart."

If, like Paul, we have mercy and a ministry we have precious resources for doing well on the gun lap. We will be able to "press on . . . because Christ Jesus has made [us] his own." Because we know we are in the firm grip of the one who spun the galaxies into being, we can run, even in bad times, with confidence.

Remember to Be Single-Minded

Paul's focus was singular: "but one thing I do . . . I press on toward the goal for the prize of the upward call of God in Christ Jesus." Earlier he had said to the Philippians, "For to me to live is Christ" (Phil. 1:21). Paul's passion was pointedly Jesus.

The race must be run with a singleness of purpose. We Christians are the people who cannot serve two masters. We are the ones who must seek first the kingdom of God. We are the ones who must deny ourselves, take up a cross, and follow Him. We are the ones who say with Paul, "One thing I do."

Our commitment, though, can be diluted by diversity. We can "spread ourselves so thin" that what commitment we have is only lukewarm. Calvin Miller told a story that is instructive:

> I remember calling for prayer requests one night. A man asked prayer for a friend. "What is the matter with your friend?" I asked. "Well," he said, he just had a gall bladder attack." I thought that a rather urgent request. He went on, "But his attack was very bad since he has been a diabetic for years." I assured him that God could heal a diabetic victim of a gall bladder attack. "Still," he continued, "his advanced leukemia may complicate things if

the doctors decide to operate." The urgency of the situation was ebbing. "The poor man," he went on, "should do all right if he survives the heart attack he had on the way to the hospital." I barely suppressed a chuckle when we got to the heart trouble. My compassion was drowned by diversity.[1]

So, too, our compassion and commitment are drowned by our diverse interests. Our lives go in so many different directions, it is impossible for us honestly to say, "One thing I do."

Certainly we should not become "ecclesiastical shut-ins," ignorant of outside activities. As I stated earlier, we Christians should be informed and intelligent. But our passion must be singular—"to live is Christ." Our heartbeat must not be the sporadic murmur of the "miscellaneous man," but the steady pounding of the "passionate man." Our world, you see, is not lacking for Christians; it is lacking for Christians who have a single aim.

Last fall, I did a fellow runner a favor. We were in the "Turkey Trot Run," an annual event put on every November by a local junior college. Toward the end of the race, this particular runner got confused as to where he was to run. He was just ahead of me, and I could see he was uncertain as to which of three roads to take. I knew we were to stay right, I yelled "go right" to him, and he promptly obeyed. Fortunately, that was the correct road, and both of us breezed in with no trouble.

His near undoing was the number of options he had. Three roads confused him. He nearly strayed from the course because he had multiple choices.

Not so with Paul. There was no confusion about which direction he would run! Wherever he went and whatever he did, the supreme goal of his life was to honor Christ, to obey Christ, to lift up Christ.

When we are facing any kind of stress or trouble, we can renew our strength if we remember *whose* we are and concentrate on Him. Running the gun lap calls us to gather our lives around a single passion.

Remember to Forget

In that same "Turkey Trot Run," I committed the unpardonable race blunder: I looked back and nearly got passed. Half a mile from the finish, a small, bow-legged woman and I were running shoulder to shoulder. Now, I don't mind getting beat by women. That happens in nearly every race I run. But this woman had terrible running form. To put it gently, she was not "fluid." She was the kind of runner that makes you mutter under your breath, "If I can't beat her I ought to quit!"

So, I stepped it up and moved ahead of her. With a hundred yards left in the "Turkey Trot," I felt smug enough to glance over my shoulder to see how much distance I had put between us. To my surprise, she had "kicked" with me! She was breathing down my neck, and I barely nipped her at the wire.

I knew better than to look back. I had even underlined Dr. Sheehan's words in *Running and Being:*

> Once in the lead, I never look back. There is no greater spur to a tired runner who is about to give up and coast in than seeing this over-the-shoulder distress signal. So I never look back. I reach for the man in front of me no matter how impossible it seems for me to catch him.[2]

But I forgot, looked back, and nearly got beaten.

Paul knew it was dangerous to look back in the race, too. He told the Philippians he was "forgetting what lies behind." No over-the-shoulder glances for Paul! His gaze was resolutely forward.

Had Paul languished in the past, he could not have written so freely of joy. "Rejoice" would not have been in his vocabulary, for he had some crippling memories. For Paul to cope victoriously in the Roman prison, "forgetting what lies behind" was crucial. He could have been overcome by depression if he had been constantly looking over his shoulder.

First, I think Paul had to forget his past sins. He could have stumbled to the finish line with the overcoat and baggage of his sinfulness. But he had stripped himself of guilt: "Where sin increased, grace abounded all the more" (Rom. 5:20). He knew that, for him, the "old" had passed away, and the "new" had come. He did not have to relive old mistakes or carry old regrets.

Second, Paul had to forget his past hurts. When we feel persecuted and are facing the strain of the gun lap, we might be encouraged to read of Paul's woes. In our misery, he can keep us good company:

> Five times I have received at the hands of the Jews the forty lashes less one. Three times I have been beaten with rods; once I was stoned. Three times I have been shipwrecked; a night and a day I have been adrift at sea; on frequent journeys, in danger from rivers, danger from robbers, danger from my own people, danger from Gentiles, danger in the city, danger in the wilderness, danger at sea, danger from false brethren; in toil and hardship, through many a sleepless night, in hunger and thirst, often without food, in cold and exposure (2 Cor. 11:24-27).

And we think we've suffered! We call the last Wednesday night business meeting persecution! Our gun lap stresses pale beside those of Paul.

But Paul had to forget those hurts lest they ferment into bitterness: "For the sake of Christ, then, I am content with weaknesses, insults, hardships, persecutions, and calamities; for when I am weak, then I am strong" (2 Cor. 12:10). By forgetting his hurts, he was able to sing of joy from the prison cell.

The third thing I think Paul had to forget was his achievement. He had achieved much in his life and had every reason to boast. He was the foremost leader in the Christian church. He had established and strengthened countless churches. He had traveled throughout the ancient world. He had sacrificed much and earned high esteem. Paul had good reason to take pride in his life. But he boasted instead of his weakness: "If I must boast, I will boast of the things that show my weakness" (2 Cor. 11:30). He was not going to sit on his laurels or glance back at his accomplishments.

Because he could leave those sins, hurts, and achievements behind him, Paul was enabled to move on in the race. If we want to do well on the gun lap, we, too, will have to remember to forget. Dragging along weights from the past will always slow us down.

Forget your sins—they have been forgiven. Forget your hurts—they will only lead to resentment. Forget your achievements—they will destroy your incentive. If you would conquer today's challenges, drop yesterday's baggage and travel light.

Remember You Have a Future

Paul didn't just forget his past. He also was "straining forward to what lies ahead." He was "press[ing] on toward the goal for the prize of the upward call of God in Christ Jesus." In other words, Paul was facing his future with expectancy.

He could have justifiably chosen to hang up his running shoes and retire to the front porch for rest. After all, he was old and battered. He had accomplished much. He was trapped in a damp prison. He had every reason to prop his feet up, heave a sigh of resignation, and quit the race.

But he didn't. He saw a future that made him "strain forward" and "press on." William Schultz has written, "If there is one statement true of every living person, it must be this: he hasn't achieved his full potential."[3] I think Paul felt that way. He still had churches to visit, people to meet, letters to write, truths to learn, and potential to realize.

Nothing motivates like a future. Viktor Frankl spent time in a Nazi concentration camp and, from that horrible experience, developed a theory of human behavior called "logotherapy." Frankl observed that those who survived the atrocities of the camp were the ones who had a *reason* to survive. They had a picture to paint, a book to write, a baby to raise, or some other purpose to fulfill. Those who felt they had a future had a stronger will to live than those without any anticipation. Frankl's logotherapy stresses the necessity of having "a reason to live and a reason to die." It accentuates the importance of having a future.

If we don't believe we have a future, it will not take a concentration camp to kill us. We will latch on to the nearest disease and die from it. Or we will stay sick most of our lives. Or perhaps we will be alive physically but comatose emotionally and spiritually. A person with no future will invariably see the race as "forced labor."

I have come to see Jesus' words to the church at Philadelphia as a promise to all Christians: "Behold, I have set before you an open door" (Rev. 3:8). Those who trust Him know there is always an open door. He has convincingly proven that even death is a door, opening into God. So those of us who know Christ do not believe any situation is a "dead end." We "strain forward" and "press on" because Christ has opened every door and redeemed every circumstance.

Knowing that we have a future and that God is working on even the darkest days will help us run the gun lap. On the far side of conflict is reconciliation. Just beyond a job loss is new opportunity. On the other side of divorce is love. After every cross is a resurrection. That is our hope and the promise of Scripture: "We know that in everything God works for good with those who love him, who are called according to his purpose" (Rom. 8:28).

Haven't you discovered the importance of a future in your own experience? Aren't you most alive when you have something to anticipate—a good book, lunch with a friend, a football game, a birthday celebration? Those future events charge us with enthusiasm and remind us how vital expectancy is to the human species. Like the people in Frankl's concentration camp, we anticipate or we die.

Paul had that anticipation. In the prison, he remembered his future and vowed to "strain forward" and "press on." Dr. Sheehan's pledge strangely echoed Paul's when he wrote:

> What do I do now? No matter what I have done, there is still more to do. No matter how well it has been done, it can still be done better. No matter how fast the race, it can still be run faster. Everything I do must be aimed at that, aimed at being a masterpiece. The things I write, the races I run, each day I live. There can be no other way.[4]

Stress is no respecter of persons. It attacks young and old, male and female, Christian and non-Christian. Everyone who walks this planet will one day have to face a gun lap that will be a test of courage and endurance.

Thankfully, those of us who are running the Christian

race have unseen resources that infuse us with energy. When we stir up the gift of memory, we remember what we have going for us: (1) We are in the firm grip of Christ, (2) we have a single-minded purpose that gives us motivation, (3) we are not shackled by our past, and (4) we know we have a future.

When we remember those resources, how can we falter?

11.
The Winner's Stand

"I have fought the good fight, I have finished the race, I have kept the faith. Henceforth there is laid up for me the crown of righteousness, which the Lord, the righteous judge, will award to me on that Day, and not only to me but also to all who have loved his appearing" (2 Tim. 4:7-8).

Second Timothy was probably Paul's last biblical letter. When he wrote it, he knew his days were numbered, that he was drawing close to the finish line. He candidly told Timothy, "I am already on the point of being sacrificed; the time of my departure has come" (2 Tim. 4:6). He spoke of his life in retrospect and exulted, "I have fought the good fight, I have finished the race, I have kept the faith" (v. 7). And he looked forward with anticipation to his trip to the winner's stand:

Henceforth there is laid up for me the crown of righteousness, which the Lord, the righteous judge, will award to me on that Day, and not only to me but also to all who have loved his appearing (v. 8).

Paul had lived with joy and enthusiasm. Even at the end of his life, he was pressing gallantly for the finish, straining forward for the heavenly prize. I thought of Paul when I read these words in Philip Yancey's book, *Where Is God When It Hurts:*

When I am old, I hope I do not die between sterile sheets, hooked up to a respirator in a germ-free environment. I hope I'm on a tennis court, straining my heart with one last septuagenarian overhead smash, or perhaps

huffing and puffing along a trail to Lower Yosemite Falls
for one last feel of the spray against my wrinkled cheek.[1]

Paul didn't want to "die between sterile sheets" either,
and all the way to the end, he was running to win.

One of John Wesley's proudest claims was, "Our people
die well." Though we do not know the factual details of
Paul's death, I believe Paul "died well." He died knowing
he had a special prize awaiting him in eternity. Let's look
at his words in 2 Timothy 4:7-8 to see what we can learn
about the winner's stand.

A Race Well-Run

Paul knew he had run well. He knew that he had fought
a good fight, run a strong race, and steadfastly kept the
faith through many trials and struggles. He had experienced disappointment, setback, and pain along the
way. He had been forced to surmount many obstacles and
jump a long succession of hurdles. But he had never lost
heart or become disenchanted with the race. Even at the
finish, he had a good "kick."

What greater joy could there be in life than that? To be
able to look back with satisfaction at the race just complet-
ed? To be able to say, "I have not betrayed Christ or lived
for trivial gods"? Surely there could be no greater ecstasy
for any of us than to look back at our personal history and
know that our lives have counted, that our days have been
brimming with God, love, and meaning.

And what greater sorrow could there be than to "die
between sterile sheets," knowing our lives have been invested in the insignificant? To die knowing that we have
missed our calling and the true purpose of our lives? It is
this dreadful possibility Dr. Sheehan alluded to when he
wrote of the necessity of heeding our "inner voice":

Our problem, then, is not the possibility of this necessity but the probability that we may never know it. That we may finish our lives without actually having lived it. That we may come to the end never having experienced it; never having heard the call. Our tragedy may be an unused soul, an unfulfilled design.[2]

With great gratitude, Paul could sing of fulfilling his design. He knew he had run the race for which he was intended. He knew he could take his place at the winner's stand with a confident smile on his face. He knew he had been faithful to the inner voice of God's Spirit.

A Crown to Be Claimed

Because he had run well, Paul expected a "crown of righteousness." No perishable wreath of laurel leaves for him! He was anticipating an imperishable prize, an eternal crown of glory given him by none other than the Pioneer and Perfecter of the faith.

We do not know all that Paul had in mind when he wrote of the "crown of righteousness," but we can assume it was a valuable prize. We can sense from these verses that whatever it was that Paul anticipated at the winner's stand, it was quite a trophy!

It doesn't take much to get me to enter a race—a T-shirt to all finishers is all the incentive I need. But don't ask me to run unless you're willing to give me one of those prized T-shirts! I will not run a race without the promise of this prize!

I used to feel guilty that I valued these shirts so much. After all, a similar shirt can be purchased at the nearest department store for about three dollars. But the more I talked to other runners, the more I realized that I was not alone in my infatuation with T-shirts. Others, too, saw them as important trophies of endurance, the uniform of the running fraternity. Listen to runners talk about a particular race and the conversation will nearly always get around to the color, style, and logo of the shirts given to participants. Dangle a good-looking, flashy T-shirt before a runner, and he'll pay his entry fee in a minute.

Paul knew that he was running for more than a T-shirt, though. All of his "pressing" and "straining" was for an incorruptible crown: "Every athlete exercises self-control in all things. They do it to receive a perishable wreath, but we an imperishable" (1 Cor. 9:25). With typical boldness and flair, Paul planned to claim his prize at the winner's stand.

A Judge to Be Trusted

There will be many questions to ask the Judge when we finally get to the winner's stand. Our minds are stuffed with big concerns about life, God, and eternity. We wish God would be more talkative now and satisfy our curiosity. Until we get to the other side, though, we wrestle with some nagging questions:

- What about the people who have never heard of Christ? How will God deal with them?
- What kind of rewards will there be in heaven?
- When, where, and how will the judgment take place?
- What good are our works when the Bible says we're saved only by God's grace?
- Is heaven really a place of golden streets and crystal rivers? Or are those images the Bible uses to describe a place that can't be described?

Those questions, and others like them, gnaw at us because we can't stand a lack of knowledge. To live in the face of such questions requires a lot of faith, and it is always hard to live by faith.

I think the best answer to those questions is this: In eternity, as in time, God is completely trustworthy. However God works those questions out, we can be assured that both grace and justice will be served. Let me remind you again of the question Abraham asked God: "Shall not the Judge of all the earth do right"? (Gen. 18:25) That question is really the wisest answer to all of our queries about eternity. God can be trusted to do what is right. Paul knew that and told Timothy that when he made it to the winner's stand, he would appear before "the righteous judge."

There was a time when "I don't know" wasn't in my vocabulary. As a seminary student, I could have given you a dogmatic answer to all of the questions listed above. But no more. Time has taught me that "I don't know" is a good answer—even for a preacher who is supposed to be the knowledgeable expert on spiritual things. I now find myself explaining God less and trusting Him more, and I think that's a part of what it means to "grow in faith."

The ancient Egyptians believed in a judgment after death and that the initial phase of that judgment was the weighing of a person's heart. Since the heart was the measure of one's courage, devotion, and love, they believed the heart had to be weighed to determine the measure of a person's life.

We Christians do not believe that God literally weighs our hearts in eternity. But what we can affirm is that, however He chooses to measure our lives, He will "weigh" us correctly. The Judge we stand before will be righteous. And, even now, we can rest our nagging questions in His dependable hands.

A Company of Celebrants

Paul knew that he had run a good race; he anticipated a crown of righteousness; and he believed that his judge could be trusted. But he also believed there would be a crowd at the winner's stand. He expected a company of celebrants to join him in claiming their prizes. He said the eternal crown would be handed "not only to me but also to all who loved his appearing." Paul saw that all of those who love Christ, who have received grace and been redeemed, will gather in great merriment at the eternal winner's stand.

Earlier, I mentioned my friend who claims runners are bent on punishing themselves. I've discovered he's not alone in his scorn for the running phenomenon. Many critics have surfaced in recent years to speak out against running. The criticisms take many forms and come from many directions—"Running is boring"; "Running is addictive"; "Running doesn't exercise the whole body"; "Running damages knees and feet"; "Running is too hard on the heart." The death of running pioneer Jim Fixx during one of his daily ten-mile runs only added fuel to the critics' fires.

Some of those criticisms bear investigation, and certainly running is not for everyone. If I had to justify the sport to these critics, though, I would list the following reasons why I daily hit the road:

(1) Running helps me feel good physically. My resting pulse is in the fifties now, and my energy level is high.

(2) Running helps me feel good emotionally. I'm convinced running drains off stress and relaxes a person.

(3) Running gives me solitude. I look forward to the daily run because I know it will be a quiet time, away from

the noisy routine, when I can collect my thoughts and pray.

(4) Running stimulates me mentally. There's something about putting the body in motion that puts the mind in motion. I get more creative thoughts "on the run" than I ever do in my study.

(5) Running teaches me discipline. The day-in, day-out regimen of running is a great teacher of perseverance and consistency.

(6) Running gives me adventure. Being able to romp through the neighborhood like a child is fun, and pitting my body against a 10-K course is a challenge.

(7) Running enrolls me in a fraternity of kindred spirits.

This last benefit bears explanation because it relates to Paul's anticipation of a company of celebrants after the race. Of all of the reasons for running listed above, this last one was the most unexpected. I had hoped that I would find the other six advantages in the sport, but I never suspected that running would introduce me to so many fine people. This fraternity of kindred spirits proved to be a real serendipity of my running experience. Many of my friends now are fellow runners, and we often talk of times, races, shoes, T-shirts, and other assorted details associated with our sport.

A few times, after an early morning race, a group of us has gathered at a local café for breakfast. There, we ate pancakes, swigged coffee, relived the race, and bragged on each other's efforts. The race was made more enjoyable because we ran it, and then celebrated it, together.

When Paul looked ahead to the winner's stand, he saw a post-race gathering of unrestrained joy. After all of the effort of the race, the participants would meet at the appointed place to collect their awards and celebrate their common love.

Every year in Boston, marathon great Bill Rodgers leads a host of runners through the streets of the city on the "Jingle Bell Run." The run is held at night during the Christmas season, and runners dress in holiday costumes, tie bells to their shoes, and shout "Merry Christmas" as they run. The run is a totally noncompetitive event, and its purpose is strictly fun and holiday merriment. At the conclusion of the 4.5-mile "Jingle Bell Run," the participants sing songs, listen to a band, eat yogurt and cake, and revel in the color and joy of the event.

Sounds like fun, doesn't it? But the "Jingle Bell Run" can't hold a candle to the post-race festivity Paul alluded to in 2 Timothy. In the Book of Revelation, John gave us an expanded picture of what to expect at the winner's stand:

> Then he showed me the river of the water of life, bright as crystal, flowing from the throne of God and of the Lamb through the middle of the street of the city; also, on either side of the river, the tree of life with its twelve kinds of fruit, yielding its fruit each month; and the leaves of the tree were for the healing of the nations. There shall no more be anything accursed, but the throne of God and of the Lamb shall be in it, and his servants shall worship him; they shall see his face, and his name shall be on their foreheads. And night shall be no more; they need no light of lamp or sun; for the Lord God will be their light, and they shall reign for ever and ever (Rev. 22:1-5).

Now, that's a party I don't want to miss! And the good news is no one has to miss it. The post-race celebration is for all who will come: "The Spirit and the Bride say, 'Come.' And let him who hears say, 'Come.' And let him who is thirsty come, let him who desires take the water of life without price" (v. 17).

Anyone who wants to can be a part of the company of celebrants in heaven. It makes you wonder, doesn't it, how anyone could refuse such an offer.

I have two children, and both are athletically inclined. My son, Randel, is a baseball star. At the ripe old age of eight, he has an uncanny gift for scooping up grounders and hitting line drives. When I watch him play, I see major league potential.

My daughter, Stacy, is ten and a fine distance runner. She runs for a local track club and has ribbons and medals plastered all over her bedroom wall. When I watch her run, I see a future Olympian.

You may want to accuse me of exaggeration and excessive parental pride. Let me assure you I have checked with their grandparents and have been told that my estimate of the children is right on target!

My fatherly exuberance nearly cost my daughter a race last summer. She was running the fifteen-hundred meters in a Junior Olympic meet. My seat in the grandstands was too far from the action, I thought, so midway through the race, I slipped out onto the field. As Stacy passed the starting line for the gun lap, I jogged along with her awhile, yelling stirring words of encouragement. If I hadn't been wearing thongs and favoring a sore knee, I probably would have run half a lap with her.

It was a good thing I didn't. An official sidled up to me after the race to let me know I had nearly gotten my daughter disqualified. No parent or coach is allowed to run with a participant, he said. Every runner in the race must run alone. All cheering must be done in the stands. Only my thongs and bad knee saved her from disqualification!

This book would not disqualify us in the race. My counsel and exhortation have, of necessity, been at a distance. We will probably never meet face to face, so this is as close as we will ever get—author with pen in hand and reader with book in lap. I would like to think I've run a few laps with you in this book, but I know better. At best, I've been in the distant grandstands, shouting to you most of what I know about the race.

Many times, as I was writing this book, I hesitated to shout at all. A book often makes the author sound like an expert on his subject. I have used a barrelful of "musts," "oughts," and "shoulds" in these pages and have sounded like a great runner in the marathon of faith. Sadly, that is not the case. To be honest, I have written these truths much easier than I live them. I am no expert on the living of the Christian life—just a runner captivated by the enormous adventure of the race. If nothing else, writing this book has impressed upon me how far I still have to go.

What it finally comes down to for all of us is this: No one can run the race for us. Parents and coaches must stay in the stands. The books, sermons, counsel, and personal relationships we have will help us and be crucial to our success in the race. But, ultimately, we run alone. We live our lives before a crowd of One. The race is run in the solitude of our personal relationship to God.

If I have, in any way, been a wise counselor or enthusiastic booster to you, I have my reward for writing this book. I hope you'll be able to flip back through these pages now and reread something you've underlined or think again about a truth that "hit home" with you.

But I also know that books don't change lives—decisions do. Only as we decide to *live* the truth in books does change occur.

Perhaps we *will* meet some day as we run the race. Maybe our paths will eventually intersect, and we will have opportunity to swap "tips" and celebrate the journey. Just in case that never happens, let's plan on meeting at the winner's stand!

Have a good run!

Notes

Chapter Two—Anticipating the Hurdles

1. Gerald Mann, *Why Does Jesus Make Me Nervous?* (Waco, Tex.: Word Books, 1980), pp.19-20.

2. Jim Wallis, *The Call to Conversion* (San Francisco: Harper & Row, 1981), p.12.

3. Soren Kierkegaard, *The Point of View for My Work as an Author*, trans. Walter Lowrie (New York: Harper & Row, 1962), pp.23-24.

4. Quoted in Richard J. Foster, *Celebration of Discipline* (San Francisco: Harper & Row, 1978), p.69.

Chapter Three—Running to Win

1. James F. Fixx, *The Complete Book of Running* (New York: Random House, 1977), p.92.

2. Ibid., p.144.

3. Frank S. Mead, ed., *Encyclopedia of Religious Quotations* (London: Peter Davis, Ltd., 1965), p.400.

4. Quoted in J. Wallace Hamilton, *What About Tomorrow?* (Old Tappan, N.J.: Fleming H. Revell, 1972), p.141.

5. Ibid., p.161.

Chapter Four—The Start

1. Eugene Peterson, *A Long Obedience in the Same Direction* (Downers Grove, Ill.: Inter-Varsity Press, 1980), p.48.

2. *Smith's Bible Dictionary* (Philadelphia: A.J. Holman Co.), p.243.

Chapter Five—Running in the Pack

1. Eugene Peterson, *Five Smooth Stones for Pastoral Work* (Atlanta: John Knox Press, 1980), p.150.

2. Robert Farrar Capon, *A Second Day* (New York: William Morrow & Co., 1980), pp.23-24.

3. George Sheehan, *Running and Being* (New York: Warner Books, 1978), p.123.

4. Peter J. Kreeft, *Heaven: The Heart's Deepest Longing* (San Francisco: Harper & Row, 1980), p.39.

5. Philip Yancey, *Open Windows* (Westchester, Ill.: Crossway Books, 1982), p.72.

6. Robert Farrar Capon, *The Third Peacock* (Garden City, N.Y.: Doubleday, 1971), pp.91-92.

7. Story told in J. Wallace Hamilton, *Who Goes There?* (Old Tappan, N.J.: Fleming H. Revell, 1958), p.69.

Chapter Six—Crowd Noise
1. Virginia Stem Owens, *The Total Image* (Grand Rapids, Mich.: William B. Eerdmans, 1980), p.5.

2. Quoted in D. Bruce Lockerbie, *The Timeless Moment* (Westchester, Ill.: Cornerstone Books, 1980), p.63.

Chapter Seven—Falling Back
1. George Sheehan, *Dr. Sheehan on Running* (New York: Bantam Books, 1975), p.8.

2. James F. Fixx, *The Complete Book of Running* (New York: Random House, 1977), p.192.

3. Lewis Smedes, *How Can It Be All Right When Everything Is All Wrong?* (San Francisco: Harper & Row, 1982), p.115.

4. Alan Sillitoe, *The Loneliness of the Long-Distance Runner* (New York: Alfred A. Knopf, 1959), p.11.

5. Joe Henderson, *Running A to Z* (Brattleboro, Vt.: Stephen Greene Press, 1983), p.173.

6. Fixx, p.207.

7. Eugene Peterson, *A Long Obedience in the Same Direction* (Downers Grove, Ill.: Inter-Varsity Press, 1980), p.111.

8. Smedes, p.115.

Chapter Eight—Second Wind
1. George Sheehan, *This Running Life* (New York: Simon & Schuster, 1980), pp.73-74.

2. George Sheehan, *Dr. Sheehan on Running,* (New York: Bantam Books, 1975), p.6.

3. Calvin Miller, *Table of Inwardness* (Downers Grove, Ill.: Inter-Varsity Press, 1984), p.35.

4. Quoted in George Sheehan, *How to Feel Great 24 Hours a Day* (New York: Simon & Schuster, 1983), p.42.

5. George Sheehan, *Running and Being*, (New York: Warner Books, 1978), p.14.

6. John Claypool, *Tracks of a Fellow Struggler* (Waco, Tex.: Word Books, 1974), pp.61-62.

7. Quoted in Tim Hansel, *When I Relax I Feel Guilty* (Elgin, Ill.: David C. Cook, 1979), p.9.

Chapter Nine—Picking Up the Pace
1. George Sheehan, *Running and Being*, (New York: Warner Books, 1978), p.35.

2. Quoted in Richard J. Foster, *Freedom of Simplicity* (San Francisco: Harper & Row, 1981), p.110.

3. Howard Taylor, *Hudson Taylor's Spiritual Secret* (Chicago: Moody Press, 1932), p.26.

4. Quoted in Foster, *Freedom of Simplicity*, p.66.

5. Ibid, p.184.

Chapter Ten—Gun Lap
1. Calvin Miller, *A View from the Fields* (Nashville: Broadman Press, 1978), p.87.

2. George Sheehan, *Running and Being*, (New York: Warren Books, 1978), p.171.

3. Quoted in Sheehan, *Dr. Sheehan on Running*, (New York: Bautain Books, 1975), p.87.

4. Sheehan, *Running and Being, p.255.*

Chapter Eleven—The Winner's Stand
1. Philip Yancey, *Where Is God When It Hurts* (Grand Rapids, Mich.: Zondervan, 1977), p.49.

2. George Sheehan, *Running and Being*, (New York: Warner Books, 1978), p.58.